# The
# Song
# Writer's
# Work
# Shop

## About the Editor

Harvey Rachlin is the author of *The Songwriter's Handbook*, *The Encyclopedia of the Music Business*, *The Songwriter's and Musician's Guide to Making Great Demos* and several other books. He is the winner of an ASCAP-Deems Taylor Award for excellence in music journalism and runs a music management company.

# The Song Writer's Work Shop

Edited by
Harvey Rachlin

Writer's
Digest
Books

Cincinnati, Ohio

**Audiotape Copyright Information:**

**Tape One:**

**Tape Two:**

## Acknowledgments

This project was conceived at Writer's Digest by Julie Whaley and supervised by Mark Garvey. Both are outstanding editors and their cachet quietly shines throughout here. I also wish to express special thanks to Michael Kerker and Dona Spangler of ASCAP, and to Lynn Chu, Glen Hartley and Judith Stein.

Thanks from Teri Muench to Randy McLeary and Shahrzad Zorba, and extra special thanks to Steve Diamond, for his invaluable help and loving support.

James Becher would like to thank his wife, MaryAnne, for all her love and support.

# Introduction
1

## JANIS IAN
# On Songwriting
3

Singer/songwriter Janis Ian discusses lyric writing, an essential element of good songwriting. Sharing her personal experiences, she gives you an extraordinary glimpse into how words, lines and ideas are shaped into lyrics with universal appeal. With exercises and lyrics.

## JOHN BARILLA
# Making Demos
23

Your demo is your strongest marketing tool. To compete you need a high-quality recording of your songs. Producer/engineer/musician John Barilla tells you all about recording equipment and production techniques that will help you create the best possible demos of your songs.

## JAMES BECHER
# Understanding MIDI
43

MIDI technology (a breakthrough in the way musical instruments communicate with each other) has far-reaching applications for songwriters. Composer/keyboardist James Becher explains the world of MIDI in simple terms and tells you how to use its benefits in your songwriting and recording.

## TERI MUENCH
# The Art of Pitching Songs
63

Once your demo is made, you face the challenge of placing it with a music publisher, record company or artist. From her insider's perspective as a record company A&R executive, producer and music publisher, Teri Muench explains the marketing process and tells you how to get your songs heard—and accepted—by the people who count in the music business.

# Glossary
77

# Index
81

# Introduction

*The Songwriter's Workshop* is a workbook and audio cassette package designed to instruct you and further your songwriting career. Four subjects are covered in this volume: Songwriting, by Janis Ian; The Art of Pitching Your Material, by Teri Muench; Making Demos, by John Barilla; and Understanding MIDI, by James Becher. Each of these topics is vitally important to the songwriter who wants to move ahead in today's world of music, and each of the authors brings to his or her subject a wealth of experience and impeccable credentials.

This package has been designed as a "portable" songwriter's workshop. In the past decade or so, songwriters' workshops have proliferated across the country, aiding songwriters tremendously in their endeavors. Songwriters' workshops serve a potpourri of functions, among which is to render expert advice to their members. There's plenty of expert advice here, and in the spirit of our "workshop," we hope you'll consider the information as personalized instruction. It's "portable" in the sense that you can use it anywhere and learn from it anytime, at your convenience. Like any course of instruction, what you get out of it is directly proportional to what you put into it.

As the computer and electronic revolutions have altered the landscape of the musical instrument and recording fields, the technique of writing tunes has likewise changed a great deal. Many of today's most successful tunesmiths have home recording studios or workshops — creative laboratories, if you will — in which they create, write and shape songs in a manner characterized more by

experimentation than linear development. They come up with musical tracks, record them, then write melodies and harmonies over them that fit the grooves. Many excellent songs have been produced in this way (just one of several techniques made possible by modern electronic equipment), but it's a bit more complicated than it sounds. One has to have a fair knowledge of the musical and recording equipment used. To maximize results, writers use an electronic patching system (to oversimplify it here) called MIDI. Having a command of techniques and technologies like these will enable you as a songwriter to expand your creative horizons, but it requires study and hands-on experience. This package will arm you with the information; it's up to you to put it into practice.

Indeed, the cassettes of *The Songwriter's Workshop* — the "tutorial" portion — could open a new avenue in your education as a songwriter. Audio offers the opportunity to demonstrate many principles and techniques that are difficult to convey with the printed word. What do *reverb* and *flanging* sound like, for example? What effects do compressors and noise gates have on sound? What does a MIDI setup sound like? How does it sound to build a song from rhythm tracks to a full-blown master? These and other questions are covered in the audio segments by John Barilla and James Becher, which permit you to hear how various tools of the trade are used to create great-sounding demos.

While the creation of music is, to varying extents, different now than in the past, the writing of lyrics has basically remained the same — both the words produced and the technique of writing them. With synthesizers, music with all different kinds of sounds can be fabricated, but words are still plain old words. (I say this with gratitude and not to disparage lyrics because, adeptly expressed, I think they can paint the most beautiful pictures.)

In *The Songwriter's Workshop*, you will learn about the craft of lyric writing from one of the most superb lyricists of our time, Janis Ian. Janis shares with you her techniques as well as some fascinating personal experiences, and she gives you exercises to hone your skill.

It would be great if, after the creation of a wonderful song, the tune automatically fell in the laps of all appropriate singers, but that of course is only wishful thinking. The reality is that it takes a lot of hard work to bring a song, even a great song, before the public. Teri Muench, who has successfully launched many original songs into Hit Heaven, tells you just how to get your tunes to the people who can make things happen.

By using the audiotapes in a "workshop" sense — listening privately, proceeding at your own rate and reviewing when you feel the need — you will maximize the value of this package. A "live" workshop offers many kinds of benefits, but what you are getting here is what is often among its best value: "personalized" instruction from the masters.

Whether you are a beginning or an intermediate songwriter, study the information here and bring it all together by putting it into practice. Practice writing lyrics (see Janis Ian's exercises), create interesting musical textures with MIDI (if you don't have the equipment, start saving and shopping around), learn how the sounds of your demos can be shaped by electronic equipment (whether you record at home or in a commercial studio). However, unless you've already established a solid track record, I'm sorry to say that no one's going to come knocking at your door for songs. You've got to be aggressive and diligent about bringing them to the attention of someone — music publisher, record producer, manager, A&R person or artist — who can get your songs out there.

Einstein came up with the formula $E = mc^2$ for the world of astrophysics. For you, the songwriter, the pertinent formula is *talent* + *practice* + *perseverance* + *aggressiveness* + *obsessive determination in all preceding elements* = *success*. It may have been easier for Einstein to create his revolutionary theory than it is for today's songwriter to get his or her tune cut, but if you've got the goods, it's really worth the effort. There are few things more wonderful in this universe than a beautiful song.

— Harvey Rachlin

# On Songwriting

## JANIS IAN

It helps to be born with a gift. Whether you call it talent, instinct or the ability to tap into the collective unconscious—whether you believe it's God-given or just that little bit of extra gray matter your parents' genes imparted—it helps. It is your gift that will make the difference between your becoming a great writer, or remaining a competent hack; between belonging to the ranks of the merely employed, or joining the aristocracy of merit.

The need for talent may seem obvious, but it's surprising how many people assume that they can write songs just because they grew up listening to the radio. Although songwriting has yet to be considered a truly "legitimate" form (being accorded much the same lack of respect that theater people once gave film writers, or film people once gave television writers), it is in fact a very difficult form to master. And quite as demanding as any of the other arts.

That's why, when younger people ask if they should "go into" songwriting as a career, most older writers will reply, "If you have any other choice, take it!" If it doesn't burn in your soul, if it doesn't *demand* to be voiced, then don't bother. You'll save yourself a lot of heartache and the rest of us a lot of time.

So the first question is: Why are you writing? Unlike other professions, the arts offer no guarantees. There are no training academies for songwriters, no apprenticeships. And there's no such thing as "If you do this and this, then that will follow." In fact, there's no security whatsoever. There's rarely even the camaraderie that working in an office setting can provide. For writers,

whose work tends to be solitary anyway, fame is usually not an option. Songwriters don't have groupies. Most listeners aren't even aware of our existence; they just assume the singer wrote the song. So if you're going for a pension or the cover of *Newsweek*, forget it right now.

Most writers who endure become writers because they must. Not to become wealthy or famous, but because they simply have no choice. Within them is a sense of something greater than themselves, something ageless and consuming, that insists on being heard. There is a longing to approach the universal, define it, and then bring it forth so that laymen can understand and enjoy it. Now admittedly, most of us don't think in those high-handed terms when we begin writing songs. We're usually just enjoying the miracle of creating something tangible out of thin air, and busy showing it off to our friends. But those who last take it a little more seriously.

This article will deal mainly with the art and craft of songwriting. We're not going into any of the peripheral aspects: pitching songs, making demos, selling or retaining publishing rights, etc. Without the song itself, none of those can exist. Likewise, we're not going to deal with commercial versus noncommercial songwriting. A good song is a good song. Period. The criteria may vary, but no one would argue that "Yummy yummy yummy I got love in my tummy" makes for deathless prose.

Anyone reading this has probably already read various books on songwriting. Most of them purport to make you a better songwriter, which usually translates into a more commercially viable production line. That's absolutely defendable. We all have to earn a living; those people who've worked a day job while their souls yearned to be creating can understand wanting to support themselves through art and art alone. But this article is not a guide to becoming self-supporting. This article is about songwriting, I hope at its best.

Because I became a professional songwriter (meaning published and recorded) at the age of fourteen, my contemporaries were always a good deal older than me. Until about four years ago I'd never even discussed writing with another songwriter. The only proper musical education I've had was eight years of classical piano lessons; I quit at eleven when my teacher slapped me for not practicing enough. I left high school in tenth grade, and words like "simile" make my eyes spin. Everything I know, from orchestral scoring to guitar chords, I either taught myself or picked up along the way. So this article is based entirely on my own personal experiences.

The foregoing paragraph is intended as a disclaimer, because it's impossible to give any advice that will always hold true. As theater people say, "The theater has no rules, and you break them at your own peril." I've watched too many great songs sit on the shelf for five years before they're "discovered"; I've seen too many good writers slog along for a decade or more until they suddenly became overnight successes. And I've heard too many truly bad songs become short-duration hits through a combination of smart politics and good timing. I don't pretend to know what will make it and what won't. But I do know a good song from a bad one, a finished work from one that's incomplete . . . and I've picked up a few things along the way.

The craft of songwriting is completely different from its adjoining arts, and yet it's no different at all. The more I've been exposed to other forms, the more astonished I've been to discover that they all follow the same basic principles. An actor's "Entrance-focus-energy-exit," a painter's use of shading, an architect's attention to the space between the columns, all apply equally well to songwriting. A great writer is very similar to a great director, or a great potter, or a great anything else. Maybe that's because they all share the same bottom line: creation.

But there are problems intrinsic to songwriting that other forms don't share. In the theater you have a multitude of voices to speak your words; body types to illustrate your characters; costumes, lighting and sets to give rhythm and a sense of place; and a director to pull it all together. In a novel, you have the luxury of time. Charles Dickens can spend two pages describing a character to us, so that when we finally meet, we already know a great deal about him. In modern poetry, there's the freedom not to rhyme, and none of the structural limitations music imposes.

In a song, you usually have three verses and one chorus to explain everything about your character, lay down a plot, develop the story, then reach some sort of resolution. Your only aid is a melody, which must be hypnotic enough to entice the listener but not so hypnotic that it dulls his ear or mind; interesting enough to keep his attention but not so interesting that he forgets about your lyric; familiar enough to keep him comfortable, but unusual enough to stand on its own against everything else he's heard. To make matters worse, the melody has got to be singable (something younger writers and most current Broadway melodists tend to forget). While a composer has the range of an entire orchestra to play with, a songwriter must be satisfied with one human voice.

In addition, you have something I can only call "invisibility." An audience doesn't listen to each new song with lyric sheets in front of them. They will hear every line only once, and they have to "get it" immediately, before the next line is upon them. You can't stop to elaborate on your text, or provide Cliff's Notes, or send your characters offstage while the audience ponders your meaning.

And on top of all that, in order for the song to be truly memorable, it has to have depth, while being couched in a manner everyone can understand. The best songs are those we can go back to again and again, finding something new each time.

Given all these problems, it's amazing that any good songs ever get written.

## Craft vs. Inspiration

There are two basic "schools" of songwriting nowadays, one based on craft, and the other based on instinct. Craft writers are those who essentially write from nine to five every day, five days a week. Instinctive writers work only "when the spirit moves them." Craft writers sometimes sneer at instinctive writers, saying they just "luck in." Instinctive writers may call craft writers assembly-line machines or hacks.

Each approach has its merits, and each has its downfall. The discipline of writing for a set amount of hours every day can bring forth unsuspected talents. Maintaining that kind of volume requires tackling a wide variety of subjects, which forces you into finding new ways to say old things. And as Don Schlitz, one of the most successful songwriters ever to hit Nashville, points out: "If you write every day, and finish everything, then when a great piece of inspiration comes along you'll be ready for it." It helps to keep your motor oiled, as it were. Staying with a difficult or boring piece of work might be the making of you; you'll have more rhymes to call on, more ways to get yourself out of tight corners. At the worst, you'll end up with a collection of stupid songs you can look back on one day with relief.

On the other hand, over a period of years the craft writer may burn out; writing then becomes a tedious chore, something to get out of the way before you can go have fun. The original reasons for being a songwriter fall by the wayside. The songs themselves become slick and hackneyed; letter-perfect, but about as enjoyable as reading the alphabet aloud. You begin to repeat yourself

or get lazy because you can get away with it.

There are also times when the river just won't be rushed. If you have patience, you may end up with a better song in the end. Craft writers sometimes depend on sheer volume to make up for what's lacking in quality. If they're unfortunate enough to be commercially successful with that volume, they can remain on the treadmill for years, creating for everyone but themselves and flooding the market with inferior material that publishers will listen to first, just because it bears their name. In that sense, they can drag us all down a level. And again, the fun can go out of it.

For the instinctive writer, there's the thrill of melding subconscious with conscious. It's magical to write that way, never knowing what will happen next, just going where the music takes you. All writers admit that they often "don't know where it came from." Some say it's in the air, or credit a deity, or say they're in touch with the collective unconscious. When someone asked the nineteenth-century French poet Charles Baudelaire where he got his inspiration, he replied, "Madame, I brush my teeth every morning." Yes, it's a facetious answer, but what else could he say? Quite often our best lines and melodies will just pop into our heads, and none of us understand how or why. Instinctive writing depends completely on that moment, so everything is a surprise. It takes the pressure of deadlines and quantity off; you count on sheer talent to provide. If you want to do an entire verse of images that don't match the chorus, you do it, and never mind whether or not anyone else can follow.

More often than not, instinctive writers are also the groundbreakers. With no rules to hold them back, and no "censor" watching over them, they often find brand new ways of saying things. If you study Bob Dylan's albums *Blonde on Blonde* and *Highway 61 Revisited*, you'll find a lot of classic examples for this kind of writing.

The problem that can arise is that instinctive writers usually don't bother paying any attention to craft; in essence, they write blind. If they're fortunate (or unfortunate) enough to have won critical or commercial acclaim it becomes very frightening. Since there's no craft to back them up, they never know if the magic will be there when they need it. That precludes ever being able to do anything involving a deadline (films, television, Broadway), co-writing on specific projects (like with an artist who's recording in two weeks) and rewriting. If you don't know how you got there in the first place, how can you change it, let alone improve on it?

As a case in point, I was fourteen when I had my first hit, a song called "Society's Child." I'd written a total of fifteen songs. Since I was also the recording artist, people identified me closely with the song itself. I woke one morning to discover that audiences twice my age were hanging on my every word. Critics would ask me to explain an abstract lyric from my album, and all I could do was smile mysteriously. Three years after "Society's Child" I left the music industry, feeling like a fraud. It wasn't until I'd written "Jesse," and then "Stars," that I felt qualified to call myself a songwriter.

Years later, discussing that period of my life with renowned acting teacher and Renaissance woman Stella Adler, I finally understood what had happened. Stella said, "Janis, you reached an age where *talent* was not enough." She was exactly right. Your talent and instinct can cover you on inspiration, but craft will see you through in the long run.

I personally believe that all art is an innate search for balance, an attempt to bring order out of chaos. To that end, I try and make use of both methods. I might undertake a specific project and enjoy the challenge of meeting a deadline. Or I might let a song sit for months, even years, because some part of me says, "You don't know how to handle this yet." Or I'll combine them, starting off with a few promising lines and religiously returning to the song two days a week until it sorts itself out.

Until you've got some years under your belt, you may not know which method serves which song best. All of us have songs that failed because we rushed to finish them, and we all have songs that will never be finished because we waited too long. Time and experience help. When I wrote "At Seventeen," I'd been a professional songwriter for over ten years. I knew I had something special after the first two lines, and I also knew it would take some time. It took four months, and I've never regretted them. In fact, I sometimes wonder if I shouldn't have taken longer.

The exasperating thing about giving all this brilliant advice is that there are always those rare, longed-for songs that just fall out. When both instinct and craft are highly honed, the work can go pretty fast. My own song "Stars" taught me that lesson. I wrote it in two hours one rainy night in Philadelphia, and it broke every rule I knew at the time. For starters, it was almost nine minutes long. The structure was free to say the least; it opened with a preamble, went directly to the chorus (which changed on each repeat), plunged into a narrative instead of a story line, and changed its melodic structure slightly every verse. To top it, you couldn't tell when the chorus might appear, sometimes after one verse, sometimes after two, and once back to back with itself. The song ended with two lines that bore little resemblance to the rest of the material; I had an afterthought the next morning and tacked it on.

None of this consciously occurred to me as I wrote; the song had (and still has) an internal logic I found acceptable. Even if it had occurred to me, I wouldn't have cared. All I really cared about was that I'd experienced something very few artists go through — stardom at such a young age — and I needed to document those years. For myself. It didn't matter that no one would record a nine-minute song, or that I had no prospect of recording it myself at the time. I didn't particularly care whether anyone else even heard the song. All I cared about was the catharsis of getting those feelings out of my heart and into music.

But . . . for three months prior to that night, I'd been trying to write a song a day, four days a week, as exercise. All my songs from that period are awful, without exception, but they gave me the facility to write a song like "Stars" in two hours. And ironically enough, it's been recorded more than any other song of mine, by artists as diverse as Cher and Mel Torme. You never can tell.

By the way, I do *not* recommend that kind of cathartic writing as a steady diet. While it's true that pain is a universal feeling, that kind of writing can be very dangerous to your career as a writer. And to you as a human being. Cannibalizing your own feelings as a sole source of inspiration can inflate your ego in desperately unhealthy ways. (For instance, by always leaving you in the victim stance, or by convincing you that the only feelings worth having are tortured ones.) It can also leave you addicted to high drama — really believing that you must suffer constantly in order to create. That's real sick. It also becomes very boring, for yourself and for your audience.

I was speaking with a hugely successful pop writer a while ago, who went on and on about how unhappy she was, how neurotic she was, how out of control her life was. I suggested she go into some sort of therapy, and she replied that she'd thought about it, but "It would remove all my reasons for writing, and all my inspiration." Don't buy into that garbage. The healthier you are in every way, the more command you'll have over your talent. Insisting that your sickness, be it alcoholism, drugs or just hanging onto your pain, actually aids your writing is a myth. It's also a cheap way to avoid taking responsibility for the guardianship of your talent.

Some artists (most of us go through it at one time or another) buy into the myth of "artist as debauchee." They point to all the great artists who've been addicts as proof. They neglect to mention that those same great artists usually died early deaths, possibly depriving us and themselves of their greatest works. I don't intend to proselytize here; most people of my generation have already gone through their addictive years. I just think it's too easy to say your talent comes from something totally outside yourself. Part of an artist's job is to nurture that talent, not to throw smoke screens around it.

## Pursuing Craft and Inspiration

How do you acquire craft? How can you hone your instincts? I've included some exercises at the end of this chapter that I hope will stimulate both, but no amount of exercise will help if you haven't done the basics. That's like trying to build a Charles Atlas body when you're still fifty pounds overweight.

The first thing is to listen to a lot of songs, and not just what's currently on the radio. Songwriting has a long and illustrious recorded history, beginning (if you really want to get technical about it) with the Greek tragedies, the Bible and countless other sources. We don't have any music available until the medieval era, when a crude notation system began to develop, but those works are worth any writer's time and effort.

At the least, try to become vaguely familiar with the great songwriters of our own century — Cole Porter, Johnny Mercer, Rodgers & Hammerstein, to name just a few. Their works may seem dated, but they had a command of language and structure that very few of us have today. Listen to their hits *and* their misses; try to figure out why some songs are hailed as classics and others never made it. Watch videos of the Broadway shows they wrote, and get those "insider's biographies" about them from your local library.

Learn to separate the song from the singer. Dylan's early work is brilliant because of his songs, even though his voice left some people cold. He's one of the most recorded songwriters of this century, because singers heard the song behind the voice. Most people listen like my friend Pat, who says, "I like songs that make me feel good about myself." Very few laymen would be as succinct as Leeds Levy, president of MCA

Publishing, who says, "I listen for the originality of the music, the universality of the lyric and the commerciality of the hook." If Pat put enough time and thought into it, she'd probably agree with Leeds. It's our job, as songwriters, to put that time and thought into our listening.

Figure out what songs you like; more important, which ones don't you like, and why. What is it about Don McLean's "Vincent" that makes so many songwriters cite it as the perfect song? Tear other people's songs apart and see if you can go them one better. Ask yourself if that song really needed a bridge, or how you'd have solved the ending. When you hear something you admire, go home and try to write it differently. Above all, be open. Anyone can learn from any form. Even something as alien to a Western ear as Noh theater music (from Japan) can teach you the value of silence.

Keep your eyes and ears open for inspiration. I wrote "At Seventeen" only because I was thumbing through the *New York Times* magazine section while idly strumming a guitar. I got interested in an article on debutantes whose lead line was something like, "I learned the truth at eighteen." (There, by the way, is where mundane day-to-day craft comes in. I was messing around with a Brazilian rhythm, and "eighteen" was too short to end the phrase, so I automatically went for a three-syllable word.) No real writer is ever bored, except by himself.

Some people get inspired by reading poetry. That's never worked for me, though seeing a great film or theater piece will often remind me that I am, in fact, a songwriter, and push me into writing.

Knowing other writers can be a help. When I started working in Nashville in 1986, at Leeds' suggestion, I came because it was the last stronghold of the songwriter. Its spirit reminded me of Greenwich Village in the 1960s. When I moved here for good, it was in large part because a community of songwriters existed. There's nothing

like singing a new song for an audience of writers, knowing they're weighing every note and comparing your song to the best of their own work. They notice every internal rhyme, every subtle twist. It's terrifying to be judged by your peers, but it sure keeps you on your toes.

Co-writing is worth looking into, especially if you feel like your writing's in a rut. It's a constant in country writing; partially to produce the quantity the industry needs, but also because someone else never thinks the same way you do. Your co-writer can turn a right angle to your normal thought process and bring something entirely new to your personal vision. If you're weak in one area, like writing catchy choruses, and lucky enough to fall in with someone strong on your missing link, I promise you'll get a lot out of it. The competitive factor may push you to greater heights, and the sheer fun of doing something that intimate with another human being can be very freeing for your solo work.

When you're a young writer, you're busy copying everyone in sight — rightly so. All artists begin as thieves; the trick is to steal well, and from the best. As time goes by you develop a distinctive style, a voice of your own. But that voice can grow dull with age. Co-writing is a good way to keep it fresh. I've learned from every single writer I've worked with, whether I was lyricist, melodist or some of each. I've also participated in some songs I will be eternally grateful for.

When I met Kye Fleming in 1986, I casually mentioned that I'd always hoped "to write another 'Jesse,' " and had never been able to. Three months later we wrote "Some People's Lives," possibly the finest song I've ever been involved with. It would never have come about on my own; the magic was that Kye and I were writing together, at that particular moment in time.

### Getting Started

The second most often asked question I get is, "How do you start a song?" (The first is, "Which comes first, the words or the music?" but since songwriters never ask that, I won't go into it here.) There are a million ways to begin. You can start with a title that will pretty much dictate the rest of the song. Or with a guitar lick, the way a lot of the early Stones songs seem to have developed. A particular rhythm (the Bo Diddley beat's always good for this). A series of chords or an instrumental pattern. Drum machines will often inspire something you can't get out of a guitar or a piano. Beginning with a concept works, too; if you have something you want to talk about but no tangible ideas for lyrics, sit down with a sheet of paper and free-associate about the subject until something comes. I've done all of the above at one time or another, to good effect. I also get a lot of ideas while driving, especially when it's a familiar route. I figure that some place in the back of my brain goes to work then, and sooner or later a melody will pop into my head, along with the start of a lyric. The important thing about starting a song is to start it. Don't be intimidated or afraid of failure. No one else ever has to hear it, but you'll learn something new every time.

How do you know which songs to finish? There is a point in your life as a writer when I believe you should finish everything; after a few years, you can afford to be more discriminating. It's usually a question of instinct. I've started songs with a couple of lines that just *felt* so right, I knew I had a good one in there somewhere.

It also depends on why you're finishing the song. If you're looking for a hit, listen to Brenda Andrews, vice-president of Almo Irving Publishing: "I know a hit when I feel it in my stomach. I always see if I can sing the melody line back to myself, if it stays with me for a while. I also think about what record buyer it could appeal to; lyrics are very important at that point."

Once you've finished your first verse and chorus, the lyric becomes even more important. You've reached the Dreaded Second Verse. Most songwriters hate reaching that point. Having fin-ished a wonderful opening, and driven home the point with a chorus, you stare blankly at the page and wonder where to take it now. One of the ways inexperienced writers destroy a promising song is to consider their second verse filler material, less important than the opening. Nothing could be further from the truth. David Conrad, also of Almo, says he always looks to see "if the second verse is as good as the first, or even better. It's no time to get lazy. That second verse might make the difference between a minor hit and one that stays charted for three months, or between a cut by an unknown singer and a cut by an estab-lished star." He's absolutely right. The song can do everything in the world for you in its opening, but that only shows its promise.

Brenda Andrews also notes that "Sixty-five percent of record buyers are women, and they're looking to hear what they want to say but can't. How they want to be treated; how they don't want to be treated." It's a good point, for two reasons. First, you have to decide whether that particular song is going to be genderless, or lim-ited to a male or female singer. More and more songwriters I know are trying to avoid tying songs down by gender; some for socio-political reasons, but most because it doubles your chances of get-ting a cut. It doesn't always work, but it's some-thing to keep in mind.

Second, any great work of art will give a voice to the voiceless. Picasso's *Guernica* is an excellent example. Painted for the Spanish Pavilion of the 1937 World's Fair, it clearly illustrated the atroci-ties committed by Franco's Fascists when they invaded Picasso's beloved Spain. The painting drew world attention to the event in a way that isolated Spanish citizenry could not.

If you examine your own favorite songs, you'll find this true: They define and solidify thoughts you've had but weren't able to express at the time. I don't care if it's Joni Mitchell's "Amelia" or "I Heard It Through the Grapevine"; the end result is the same.

## Some Songwriting Rules

### Rhymes

There are a few basic rules, which most of us learn through trial and error. Does it rhyme? A rhyme scheme helps to hypnotize, to force its way into our listening selves, much the same as African drums or Gregorian chants will. Internal rhymes can intensify the effect. Dylan's "It's All Right, Ma (I'm Only Bleeding)" is a brilliant example of assaulting the listener with a barrage of internal and external rhymes that work because they're controlled by a master writer.

Some lyricists are very picky about this subject, insisting that every line must rhyme with something. I don't agree. Most of the time they must, but sometimes the lack of a rhyme can emphasize a line much better than having a rhyme. Lyricists can also get finicky about "pure" rhymes (rhyming "time" with "sublime," rather than rhyming "time" with "wine"). I think that's carrying a good thing too far. Try it out loud; if it sounds right to your ear, it probably works just fine. But don't get carried away. There's a famous story of a songwriter who rhymed "can't" with "paint." It worked, because of her pronunciation, but only because she was also the recording artist.

Some people insist on continuing a first-verse rhyme pattern through the entire song, without deviation. In other words, if you've rhymed line one with line two, and line three with line four (an "A-A-B-B" rhyme scheme), you can't break that pattern in the next verse. I personally find that melodies usually dictate their rhyme schemes pretty well without my interference. And I'm a big fan of changing them when I need the flexibility. But that's me.

### Consider the singer

Be aware of singers' problems. They have to breathe, and at reasonable intervals. You can't ask them to gasp for air and plunge right back into the lyric. It's also very difficult to start off on a high note, without anything leading up to it for support. Certain vowels will sing better on high notes than others. "Oh" is difficult to hit at the top of your range. "Eee" is easier, and "Iii" lets the singer do even more with the vowel sound. Michael Jackson's a wizard at knowing which vowels work best where for his own vocal range. I'm a big fan of singing out loud when I write, or trying it on my co-writer's voice. It doesn't matter if you both sound awful; singing lets you monitor how difficult it'll be for someone else to sing.

Can you change the tempo and still make it work? Sometimes that's a good gauge of how flexible (or recordable) a song will be. If it's too dense (lyrics and/or melody packed in too tightly), upping the tempo a hair will make it unsingable.

### Work on your weaknesses

Exercise your weakest areas. They'll grow easy to identify. If everyone seems excited but loses interest midway through the chorus, song after song, you've got a problem with choruses. If people never seem to "get" what you're driving at in your wrap-up, concentrate on being clearer. If attention seems to wander through all your songs, get rid of the excess baggage and tighten up your lyric. These are all problems that won't resolve themselves without some work on your part. Rewrite the chorus five times if you have to — or replace it with four others. Even if you go back to the original, you'll have stretched your muscles.

I was writing with Don Schlitz one day when he accused me of being unable to write a three-chord song. Not only was I embarrassed, I was also challenged. (Particularly when I discovered that I avoided not only three-chord songs, but four- and five-chord songs as well.) I went home and wrote a song called "Days Like These," now one of my favorites. It has three chords. Limiting your knowledge in that way forces you to learn new things.

### Your ideas

Watch your basic concepts. Almost every idea has been used before — are you doing it better, or at least differently? And while you don't have to live through everything you write about, don't be stupid, either. If you grew up in a Beverly Hills mansion, you're going to have a hard time writing about strip mining in Kentucky.

## Condescension

Beware of condescension, musically and lyrically. The easiest-looking forms are usually the hardest. Again, country music is a good example. Lots of pop writers have tried to break into this field, assuming that because the songs appear simple, they're easy to write. Almost none of those writers have succeeded, because they've ignored two essential things. One, country songs have to feel authentic, and when someone like me tries to write a song that sounds like it sprang full-grown from Bucksnort, Tennessee, it just doesn't fly. Two, the best country songs can afford to sound simple because they're not. The lyrics are terse, without a wasted line; every single word is necessary.

The same holds true for jazz, classical, dance or any other form. Don't jump on the bandwagon just because that's what's selling right now. It doesn't hurt to try those forms, but have some respect for their history before you try to pass yourself off as an authority. Imitation may be the sincerest form of flattery, but it's still imitation. Try not to discount a form as beneath you, or childish, until you've mastered it.

## Story songs

If you're writing a story song (probably the most difficult song form to master), it had better be a good story, with a beginning, a middle, an end and some drama in between. The characters must be real to us immediately, provoking our sympathy (or at least empathy) within the first verse. I cannot overemphasize the need for drama here; after all, who's interested in a story that has no plot?

The Don Henry/John Vezner song "Where've You Been" (see page 19) is a classic example of this genre. In three short verses, a four-line chorus and a bridge, they relate the story of two lives from youth through old age and infirmity. The song has everything a great story song requires— a very singable melody, interesting enough to stand on its own—a dramatic beginning and ending—a second verse that furthers the narrative and adds to our understanding of the characters and their relationship—and a twist, starting at the bridge, that makes the song universal to our times, while remaining faithful to its own uniqueness. The bridge, both musically and lyrically, greatly strengthens the power of their last verse and chorus. To top it all, the song is so sparse that it never descends into the maudlin. If you're going to write story songs, have something to say.

## Metaphor

Mixed metaphors are another thing most of us have to conquer. For instance, if your song begins by comparing life to a garden, you'll try and stick with images that fit the metaphor: rain, earth, flowers, etc. But if you use the garden metaphor in your first verse, then begin talking about accounting at the chorus, people will become confused. And the cardinal rule is "Don't confuse your audience."

For instance, in my song "Stars" (see page 19), the metaphor of a star worked well partly because it accomplished a dual purpose: It's a nature image that everyone is familiar with, as well as a Hollywood film image most people know. So when my chorus went, "Stars, they come and go / they come fast or slow / they go like the last light of the sun / all in a blaze / and all you see is glory," most people understood it on both levels without much work. But in the body of the song, I had to be careful to stick with one meaning or the other; if I'd skipped around too much, the song would have lost its thread. Were I writing it now, I'd probably close with lines that would try to bring the entire image back to its original intent.

Likewise, beware of overusing a metaphor.

Some concepts are just too small to carry an entire song. How much can you get out of a particular image? If it's not enough to carry three verses, don't use it, or fill the spaces around it judiciously. Don't flog it to death until we're all praying for the song to end. Stella Adler tells young actors, "Your talent lies in your choices." That's even truer for us.

Slogans present the same problems as overused metaphors, with an additional complication: Most slogans carry a political overtone, and people tire of them rapidly. It's hard enough to tackle a trendy subject like ecology in a way that will make people respond. To add an overused phrase like "Save the whales" virtually guarantees their inattention from that moment on.

### Overtones

That brings us to another area songwriters are hyperaware of—overtones. Instrumentally, overtones are the excess notes your ear hears after registering the main note. Technically, an overtone is "an additional, usually subsidiary and implicit, meaning or quality" (*Random House College Dictionary*). Words and music both carry specific overtones. Everyone has songs or records that open up the floodgates of memory; you hear them and are suddenly transported back in time. In the same way, certain words carry specific images around them, whether or not we're consciously aware of it. "Freedom" is a loaded word, difficult to use well because we associate so many different experiences with it. Try free-associating sometime with a word like that; it recalls everything from reciting the pledge of allegiance in fifth grade to reading about a foreign war to breaking up with a lover to leaving your parents' home, and on and on and on. Your listener is making those associations too, on some level.

To illustrate: My own current favorite song is called "Tattoo" (see page 20), about the survivor of a concentration camp. It gets a standing ovation nearly every show. I had been wanting to write about the subject for years; I'd even done

library research to see how other writers had handled it. In the entire song, I never mention any of the words normally associated with it: "Nazi," "war," "camp" and the like. The song works so well in large part because I avoided images that might carry overtones of force-fed history lessons, or gruesome photographs. Instead, I paid vivid attention to my personal images, to what would move *me* the most. Its key line is in the bridge, when the female character says, "I have never loved a man . . . what man will want me now?" I hit the word "now" on a high note, to give it emphasis, then insert a full two bars before the next lyric, giving my listeners time to absorb.

There are lots of reasons why, at that moment, every man in the audience suddenly sits up, and all the women shudder. In two lines, I've told them that the character is a virgin, that she's young, that she's never been in love—and that she's either been raped or disfigured in some way. On a subconscious level, we know that she's been deprived of everything she expected to get out of life: marriage, a home, children. In essence, she's lost her future. I don't expect the audience to realize all of that in fifteen seconds, but it goes in somewhere, and they respond viscerally to the overtones.

So pay attention to your own unconscious images. There's a world of difference between "she walked" and "she strolled," between "I miss you" and "I long for you."

It's also nearly impossible to use "curse words" without making your listener uncomfortable (which may be your intent) or angry (ditto). I recently watched a young songwriter open his audition with the line "The bitch got gangbanged," hoping to attract attention. Not only did he alienate everyone in the audience—he looked like an idiot. We assumed he didn't have the talent to write a memorable song without using that kind of sledgehammer approach.

On her album *Broken English*, Marianne Faithfull does a stellar job of using every trashy word in the book to drive home her character's anger and sense of futility. That's about the only time I've heard it work.

Overtones hold true for music as well as lyrics. You can't use a slow samba feel without evoking sensuality and the tropics, or three-quarter time without echoing a waltz. This holds true for instrumentation also; distorted guitars sound out of place on folk ballads, and flutes are silly on a heavy metal demo most of the time, since they conjure memories of classical music.

Here are some other things I often hear when listening to younger writers:

*Word repetition.* Repeating a word like "miracle" in the same verse, let alone the same line, is a no-no. If you're not creative enough to find a substitute, you shouldn't be writing about that word in the first place. It's awful when someone takes an overused word like "heart" and rhymes it with itself. Repetition can work for hypnotic effect, but almost anything else sounds like lazy writing.

*Bad or esoteric titles.* You want people to remember the title so they can ask to record that song or go out and buy a copy of the record it's on. I had a song I'd titled "Stealing Fire," but audience members kept referring to it as "Stolen Fire," so I changed the title. In the sixties, it was very in vogue to give songs titles that had nothing to do with the lyrics. We're over that now. Even musically: There's a reason Beethoven's Opus 27, no. 2 is known to most of us simply as "The Moonlight Sonata." It's easier to remember.

*Concept repetition.* So you have a great opening verse about how it feels to buy your first car. And in your second verse you talk about how it felt to buy your first car. Again, that's just lazy writing. A song should develop, like a novel. Newspaper articles are wonderful examples of terse, clean language; they get the basic ideas across in the first paragraph, then elaborate on them through the rest of the piece, ending with a "wrap." Journalists understand the concept of a title, lead line, opening narrative, hook and summation better than most songwriters. Like

the actor's "Entrance-focus-energy-exit," most songs share a basic structure because that basic structure *works*. So avoid repeating yourself; with only three or four minutes available, you need every new line you can get.

Another problem is *unnecessary words*. They're just that: unnecessary. Inexperienced writers will throw a couple of words in just to make a line scan with the melody from the previous verse. Change the melody—shorten it, elongate a vowel sound, anything—but don't waste time. Listeners have changed over the last fifty years. Just look at movies and television. In the forties, when someone was going to discover a dead body, we watched him pull up to the house, get out of the car, walk up the front steps, open the door, go through the house and find the body. Nowadays we see him pull up to the house, then cut to him finding the body. Quite a difference! People are used to filling in the blanks; it's hard for them to slow down. Wasted words are a luxury you cannot afford.

Avoid *awkward writing*, like reversing a phrase just to make it rhyme. For instance, "Far across a sun-drenched brook / Into your amber eyes I look." You can't suddenly throw elevated English like that into an otherwise common song. Most modern songs are conversational; even melodically, they tend to follow the vocal patterns we use when speaking. It would be jarring if you were in the middle of a heated discussion and suddenly broke into Shakespearean English. The same holds true for songs.

*Clichés* become clichés because they're true, but they also become too familiar to move us. Try to be original with your descriptions and rhymes. Almost no one can get away with "moon/spoon/June" anymore. Still, I heard a girl singing at the Bluebird Cafe who used just those words and made them work. The truth of her feelings shone through all the trite phrases she used; her song was so simple and heartfelt that we gave her an ovation. Authenticity in lyrics counts for a lot;

you can't buy it, and you can't learn it, but you can certainly make use of it.

Of course the best songs, like the best of anything, usually break most of the rules I've just mentioned.

## Rewriting

Learning to rewrite is a painfully acquired craft. Becoming a good editor is even harder than becoming a good songwriter. As a writer, you can depend a lot on your subconscious: the phrase that comes out of nowhere, the instinctive feeling that something "just doesn't work." It's even enjoyable to edit as you write, because you're in the midst of creating the song. But once that song is "finished," rewriting can be an intensely painful process. Still, you have to learn to do it. The song itself may not work, while the idea is still great. An artist or publisher may request a change; a director may need to "lose" twenty seconds of your piece to fit his film cut. You have to live with throwing away "the best line in the whole song" because it's sitting in a bridge that doesn't flow. Or throw out a chorus you're in love with, because it doesn't lock with the rest of the song.

My advice is to develop a ruthless streak. When you've finished the song, make a tape or a clean lyric sheet. Get away from it for a while—a day, a month—however long it takes for you to become less attached. Then look long and hard. Poke holes in it. Sneer; think of what a cruel reviewer would say. Does it move you? Are there spots that make you uncomfortable, with the gnawing feeling that something's missing? Does the bridge bore you? Try and look at it through different eyes: what would a singer say? a publisher? most of all, a disinterested listener? Sure, *you* know what you meant in that verse—will they?

I've watched an incredible number of songwriters (including myself) defend an abstract passage that appears in the middle of nowhere by going into a fifteen-minute explanation. Forget it. You've got about twenty seconds to grab your listener's limited attention, and an average of three minutes to make a lasting impression. No one cares what you meant when you wrote it; they care what they *feel* when they hear it.

Take your time. It's too easy to let a half-finished song go out because you're excited over its potential. God help the writer who tells a publisher, "It really isn't finished yet, but you get the general idea." Would you do that to an audience? No one's interested in your rehearsals. If a publisher gets two or three tapes like that, she won't bother listening to your next effort. Part of building a life as a songwriter is building a reputation. Whether it's for depth or for danceability doesn't really matter; you want people to respect your work enough to listen the next time. So be fairly sure about what you're offering.

When people tell me they're budding songwriters, my first question is always "Are you any good?" If they say "Gosh, I dunno," or look dubious and wait to get their necks out of the noose, I lose interest. If you're not sure, don't write. Don't take up anyone's time or patience. Self-confidence is half of success; when you don't have it, fake it. A good song is a good song, and if you don't know one by now, get out of the business. They'll murder you out there.

Speaking of murder, learn to hear criticism with a smile. Not only will you pick up the occasional bit of sense, but it'll help you live longer. I'm not saying that you should take abuse; you'll quickly find out who can be trusted. There are publishers who insist on rewrites until every bit of heart has disappeared and the song is ruined. You have the right to ask them to step aside before it reaches that point. Nor do I mean to go against your own best judgment. I've been called everything from "the greatest female writer of our generation" (*N.Y. Times*) to "a short, pudgy woman who meanders aimlessly" (*London Times*). Some days it just doesn't pay to listen. But honest criticism can work wonders. As a serious, practicing songwriter, you're no longer part of the lay public, yet you're writing for their ears. So when someone says, "I don't get it," look again. Maybe you're too close.

I've developed a group of people whose opinions I trust, ranging from my business manager to a waitress at the local Shoney's. Each has a completely different point of view, and each has something valid to offer. But ultimately, if my waitress friend isn't moved, I worry. In general, the best people to depend on for criticism (other than the ideal: a brilliant songwriter, extremely articulate, whose work you admire, and who happens to have loads of free time) are laymen. They are, after all, the people who'll be buying the song. It's fine to be known as a "songwriter's songwriter," but it's awfully hard to earn a living that way. And the great songwriters—Leonard Cohen, for instance—have both; songwriters learn from them, and laymen listen.

I began "Jesse" (see page 21) as a song about a Vietnam vet who was missing in action. There were lots of things I wanted to say about him to give the name substance, to "put a face on him." Eventually I realized that the song wasn't about Jesse so much as it was about the woman singing to him. I also realized that the Vietnam issue would limit the song to one specific time period. At that point I trashed the second verse and started all over again. Hopefully, with time and experience, the bulk of your rewriting will come automatically with the initial creative step. Still, I'm constantly humbled when I double-check last year's work and realize how little I knew then.

Remember also that it's easier for a listener to identify with one person than with two; with two rather than a group. If you're dealing with one or two people, you can make them into archetypes for an entire class or nation, but it's hard to get people worked up about either without a human they can identify with. Anyone would rather read a novel than a page of statistics. About the only exception to that is when you're dealing with a country by name, or a religious preference. Again though, countries and religions are loaded images, and difficult to translate.

Which brings us to another bane of the songwriter—accessibility. Are you content for your song to be meaningful only to the Male Catholic Vegetarian Backpacker's Society of Santa Monica? Fine. Do you even care whether it can be translated into another language or understood in the South as well as the North? Everyone knows what the Civil War was, but Northerners will not understand if it's referred to as "The War of Northern Aggression." Similarly, on hearing "The War," most Northerners think of World War II; most Southerners are thinking of the War Between the States, or the Civil War.

My personal goal is to reach the largest number of people possible, without going against my own grain. That may require compromise (a much-misused word that carries negative connotations nowadays), but there's a big difference between compromising a metaphor and compromising your integrity.

When Kye and I wrote "What About the Love," we knew that in taking on organized Christianity we were limiting the song, probably to the United States, possibly to a liberal audience. We tried to make it more accessible by using universal images—Wall Street, old age, the cross—but we still felt it would be limited by its subject matter. However, Amy Grant recorded it, and it's done very well overseas. So you can never be sure. Just be conscious.

## Hurdles to Overcome

The most common problem once you've learned your craft is Fear of Failure. It comes in two forms. Fear of Failure #1 is the daily struggle—can I write? Do I have anything left to say? Will anybody listen? Do I care? It usually appears just before you write something wonderful. In its more nauseating form, it may hang around for weeks or months. Everything you think of is boring, stupid, not up to your standards.

My advice when this hits is to treat it like a cold. At the beginning, try to ignore it. Go on about your work pretending it doesn't exist. You may surprise yourself. If it drags on longer than a couple of weeks, stop trying. Go to the movies; take time off. Maybe you've been writing too much and you're burned out; get stimulated by something other than your work for a while. TALK to people. Relate to the world. Get away from music and take the pressure off. Deadlines are fine and most of us thrive on them; unrelenting twenty-four-hour-a-day pressure, month after month, is deadly in any situation.

Above all, don't let anyone beat you up about it. No one needs to hear, "Written anything new?" every single day, or have another writer exclaim, "You've only written (ten-twenty-eighty) songs so far this year!?" Most of us have enough problems learning not to diminish ourselves; we don't need any help. Explain this to friends and family if you have to, but don't live with it.

If the block becomes chronic—if you've been writing just fine for two years, and three months go by with nothing coming out—consider other sources. Are you physically ill? tired? drinking too much? falling in love? breaking up? Maybe you're just busy experiencing things and collating them somewhere in the back of your brain.

If all else fails, try therapy. Writer's block is something we all avoid speaking about, as though we could jinx ourselves. Still, no one knows 100 percent of what's going on in there. A good therapist can help you get clear. And since as writers we're usually very articulate, and we love talking about ourselves, it can be a lot of fun for all concerned.

Fear of Failure #2 comes when the only place to look is down. This is a rarer problem; it waits to attack until you're successful. Note that I didn't say "commercially successful." I mean any success, from having a number-one record to writing what you feel is the perfect song. Every writer I know has that one brilliant moment: Everyone else agrees that it's perfect, no one fails to be moved on hearing it, and you live on the high of your creation and their response for a few golden weeks. Until . . . suddenly you begin to wonder if it was a fluke. Maybe you just got lucky; maybe you used up all your talent in that one shot. The doubt grows, and you wonder if you'll ever write anything as good again—or even write something adequate.

This leads straight into the Fear of Failure #1 cycle, with additional pressure. If your success was commercial, the publisher, record company, singer will be wondering the same thing you're asking yourself—can you do it again?

In consolation, every artist in the world goes through it. And the only thing that can reassure you is time: time, and creation. But remember this. Songs do *not* appear out of thin air. Their inspiration may, but the song itself was the result of your talent and your ability to use the craft. If you did it once, you can do it again. Someday. So don't give up.

The flip side of Fear of Failure, for me, is the Brick Wall Syndrome. That's when you feel as if every corner you turn leads smack into a brick wall, and you never see it in time to avoid smashing your nose. It hurts. Badly. Doors slam in your face, people won't return your calls; if you've been commercially successful, gas station attendants may ask, "Are you still doing music?"

I always thought I'd reach a point in my career where every door would open, every publisher would want me, and my name would be on every singer's lips. There's no such thing. If Marlon Brando had to audition for *The Godfather*, how can I complain? We all have doors slam in our faces. The only advantage to a long career is that you get a little used to it. Not much, but a little.

When I was fourteen and running around with "Society's Child," someone at Elektra Records said, "You'll never be a successful singer; devote yourself to writing. That's where all your talent lies." The same day, a famous manager who handled most of my favorite acts told me I'd never make it as a writer and should concentrate on singing. In a way I was lucky; I learned young that two very respected authorities in my field could disagree about me completely. Caught between a rock and a hard place, my only option was to trust my own instincts. And that's the best advice for anyone. If doors slam, go around them; when walls loom, learn to dig under. But don't let anyone squash you. Writing without the support of publisher, artist, record company, club owner, manager is frightening, and having no outlet for your work can make you feel like you're writing in a vacuum—but it's better than not writing at all.

As a sidelight, let me close with this story. Kye and I wrote "Some People's Lives" (see page 21) in four backbreaking days. We literally walked, talked, and ate the song, working in the car, in restaurants, even at a social brunch her publisher had prepared. Something told us that if we didn't sit on it, the song would get away from us. At the time, Kye was signed to Almo and I was with MCA. When we finally finished, we did something neither of us had done before; we called our publishers and asked if they would see us immediately. On the way to Almo, I pulled over and we both said out loud "Are we crazy? Is this song any good?" We were experienced enough to know that sometimes you lose the forest for the trees.

We played it for Lance Freed and Brenda Andrews first. Their reactions were all we could hope for; Lance even teared up, saying, "That's a work song" (meaning it would take time and effort to get it cut), "but it's a great song. If you bring me one of those a year, it'd be plenty." When we played it half an hour later for Leeds Levy and Rick Shoemaker, their reaction was identical. Kye and I walked away thinking we were the greatest thing since sliced bread.

But "Some People's Lives," although it was submitted to nearly every ballad singer in the industry during 1986, was cut by only one: Michael Johnson, often called a "writer's singer" because of his willingness to make difficult material his own. Some singers, like Anita Baker, were nice enough to call and tell us the song was brilliant but didn't suit the direction of their album. Most just ignored it. Kye and I went in and out of being totally discouraged, reassuring one another that it was just a matter of time.

Four years later, in 1990, the song is suddenly hitting its stride, with record company A&R people picking it for Anne Murray and Barbra Streisand, and with Bette Midler actually recording it. That's the reason Leeds and Lance were so excited—because the song is what's known as "a copyright." I hope it will be played and recorded by a lot of different people over a long period of time, generating income for the publishers and writers over several decades. Incidentally, longevity usually brings higher earnings in the long run. "White Christmas," "Moon River," "As Time Goes By"—those were all "work songs," and they're all still earning everyone a very good living. More important, new generations of listeners are discovering them.

So remember that when you get discouraged. "Over the Rainbow" was nearly left out of *The Wizard of Oz* because the front office felt it was too maudlin. There are a thousand stories of songs that made the rounds for years, until they finally reached an artist daring enough to take a chance. Those are usually the songs that endure.

Nashville, June 1990

## Some Uncommon Exercises

1. Pick a song you envy, one that you wish you'd written.

    a) Write a different lyric to the same melody.

    b) Write a different melody to the same lyric.

    c) Write a different song, using the same concept.

2. Rent films that have no "title song"; most of the older classics just used orchestration. A couple I've worked with are *Night of the Hunter* and *To Kill a Mockingbird*.

    a) Write the title song, using the film title in it somewhere.

    b) Write a song that could play at the end of the film, using your favorite character's viewpoint. Not the main character, but your favorite.

c) Write the same song from another character's viewpoint. For instance, with *Night of the Hunter*, you could write first from the little boy's perspective, and then from Robert Mitchum's.

3. Pick three nouns (like "wall," "tree" and "popcorn"). Write a song that centers around each noun. Try to use metaphors.

4. Write a new theme for your favorite television show.

5. Write some parodies, of your own or other people's work. My band (Chad Watson, Jim Brock, Robert Haynes) and I wrote an entire version of "Tattoo" called "Tabu," that began with "her new scent was sprayed across her wrist / It was stronger than the old one." It forces you to detach.

6. Write several waltzes, just to get the feel.

7. Take a walk and then write what you saw. Do NOT try to take an "interesting" walk.

8. Write a song that needs no chorus.

9. Write a song that begins with its chorus.

10. Pick your least favorite song. Rewrite it so that, in your opinion, it's at least good.

11. Listen to the following and try to copy the style of each song by writing one of your own:

Hank Williams: "I'm So Lonesome I Could Cry"

Rolling Stones: "Satisfaction" and "Let's Spend the Night Together"

Everly Brothers: "Wake Up Little Susie" and "Bye Bye Love"

Bob Dylan: "Blowin' In the Wind" and "Desolation Row"

The Beatles: "Yesterday" and "I Want to Hold Your Hand"

Any two songs by Chuck Berry

Ella Fitzgerald: "Take the A Train"

Nina Simone: "Four Women"

If you can't find these at your local library or borrow them from friends, pick other songs by the same people. Just make sure the styles are different from your own.

## Discography and Suggested Reading

BOB DYLAN: *Bringing It All Back Home* (includes "It's All Right, Ma"), *Blonde on Blonde*, *Highway 61 Revisited*, all on Columbia Records.

JANIS IAN: *Janis Ian* (includes "Society's Child") Polygram Records. *Stars* (includes "Jesse" and "Stars") and *Between the Lines* (includes "At Seventeen") on Columbia Records.

JONI MITCHELL: *Hejira* (includes "Amelia") on Asylum Records.

KATHY MATTEA: *Willow in the Wind* (includes "Where've You Been") on Polygram Records.

MARIANNE FAITHFULL: *Broken English*, on Island Records.

AMY GRANT: *Lead Me On* (includes "What About the Love") on A&M Records.

MICHAEL JOHNSON: *That's That* (includes "Some People's Lives") on RCA Records.

DON MCLEAN: *American Pie* (includes "Vincent" ["Starry Starry Night"]) on United Artists.

STELLA ADLER: *The Technique of Acting*, Bantam Books, 1988.

I would strongly suggest that any writer seriously explore other literary forms, particularly novels and biographies of other writers. A few that have helped me are:

*The Day on Fire* (a life of Arthur Rimbaud) by James Ramsey Ullman. This may be out of print by now, but it's worth hunting for.

*Prince of Tides* by Pat Conroy

*My Name is Asher Lev* by Chaim Potok

*The Notebooks of Dylan Thomas* in New Directions

The Norton Critical Editions and Norton Anthologies are also invaluable sources of inspiration and knowledge.

## WHERE'VE YOU BEEN

Claire had all but given up
when she and Edwin fell in love
She touched his face
and shook her head
In disbelief she sighed and said
In many dreams I've held you near
but now at last you're really here

    Where've you been
    I've looked for you forever and a day
    Where've you been
    I'm just not myself when you're away

He asked her for her hand for life
and she became a salesman's wife
He was home at night by eight
but one stormy evening he was late
Her frightened tears fell to the floor
until his key turned in the door

    Where've you been
    I've looked for you forever and a day
    Where've you been
    I'm just not myself when you're away

        They never spent a night apart
        For sixty years she heard him snore
        Now they're in a hospital
        in separate beds on different floors

Claire soon lost her memory
Forgot the names of family
She never spoke a word again
Then one day they wheeled him in
He held her hand and stroked her head
In a fragile voice she said

    Where've you been
    I've looked for you forever and a day
    Where've you been
    I'm just not myself when you're away
    No, I'm just not myself when you're away

## STARS

I was never one for singing
what I really feel
except tonight I'm bringing
everything I know that's real

    Stars, they come and go
    they come fast or slow
    they go like the last light of the sun
    all in a blaze, and all you see is glory
    Hey but it gets lonely here
    when there's no one here to share
    I can shake it away
    if you'll hear a story

People lust for fame
Like athletes in a game
we break our collarbones and come up swinging
Some of us are downed
Some of us are crowned
and some are lost and never found
But most have seen it all
They live their lives in sad cafes and music halls
They always come up singing

Some make it when they're young
before the world has done its dirty job
and later on, someone will say
You've had your day
You must make way
But they'll never know the pain
of living with a name you never owned
or the many years forgetting what you know too well
That the ones who gave the crown
have been let down
You try to make amends
without defending

Perhaps pretending you never saw the eyes
of grown men of twenty-five
that followed as you walked
and asked for autographs
or kissed you on the cheek
and you never could believe they really loved you

Some make it when they're old
Perhaps they have a soul they're not afraid to bare

Or perhaps there's nothing there

> Stars, they come and go
> they come fast, they come slow
> and they go like the last light of the sun
> all in a haze, and all you see is glory
> But some have seen it all
> They live their lives in sad cafes and music halls
> They always have a story

Some women have a body men will want to see
and so they put it on display
Some people play a fine guitar
I could listen to them play all day
Some ladies really move across a stage
and gee, they sure can dance
I guess I could learn how
if I gave it half a chance
But I always feel so funny
when my body tries to soar
And I seem to always worry
about missing the next chord
I guess there isn't anything
to put up on display
except the tune, and whatever else I say
And anyway, that isn't really
what I meant to say
I meant to tell a story
I live from day to day

> Stars, they come and go
> they come fast, they come slow
> and they go like the last light of the sun
> all in a haze, and all you see is glory
> But some have seen it all
> They live their lives in sad cafes and music halls
> They always have a story
> So if you don't lose patience
> with my fumbling around
> I'll come up singing for you
> even when I'm downed

## TATTOO

Her new name was tattooed to her wrist
It was longer than the old one
Sealed in the silence with a fist
This night will be a cold one
Centuries live in her eyes
Destiny laughs over jack-booted thighs
"Work makes us free," says the sign
Nothing leaves here alive
Tattoo

She steps out of line to the left
and her father to the right
One side's a cold, clean death
The other is an endless night
Gold from a grandmother's tooth
Mountains of jewelry and toys
piled in the corners, mailed across the borders
Presents for the girls and boys
Presents for the girls and boys
Tattoo

> And it gets darker every night
> Spread-eagled out among the stars
> she says "Somewhere in this tunnel
> lives a light—still my beating heart
> I have never known a man
> What man will want me now?
> Am I still alive somehow?
> If I can survive somehow,
> tattooed"

Soldiers from the other side
liberated them at dawn
Gave her water, gave her life
She still had all her clothes on
She lived until she died
empty as the autumn leaves that fly
Surgeons took the mark,
but they could not take it far
It was written on her heart
Written on her empty heart
Tattooed

The Songwriter's Workshop

## JESSE

Jesse, come home
There's a hole in the bed
where we slept
Now it's growing cold
Hey Jesse, your face
in the place where we lay
by the hearth, all apart
It hangs on my heart

    And I'm leaving a light on the stairs
    No, I'm not scared
    I wait for you
    Hey Jesse, I'm lonely
    Come home

Jesse, the floors and the boards
recalling your step,
and I remember too
All the pictures are fading
and shaded in gray
but I still set a place
on the table at noon

    And I'm leaving a light on the stairs
    No, I'm not scared
    I wait for you
    Hey Jesse, I'm lonely
    Come home

Jesse, the spread on the bed
is like when you left
I've kept it up for you
And all the blues and the greens
have been recently cleaned
and they're seemingly new
Hey Jes, me and you

    We'll swallow the light on the stairs
    We'll do up my hair
    We'll sleep unaware
    Hey Jesse, I'm lonely
    Come home

## SOME PEOPLE'S LIVES

Some people's lives
run down like clocks
One day they stop
That's all they've got
Some lives wear out
like old tennis shoes
no one can use
It's sad, but it's true

    Didn't anybody tell them
    Didn't anybody see
    Didn't anybody love them
    like you love me

Some people's eyes
fade like their dreams
Too tired to rise
Too tired to sleep
Some people laugh
when they need to cry
and they never know why

    Doesn't anybody tell them
    that's not how it has to be
    Doesn't anybody love them
    like you love me

        Some people ask
        if the tears have to fall
        then why take your chances
        Why bother at all

And some people's lives
are as cold as their lips
They just need to be kissed

    Didn't anybody tell them
    Didn't anybody see
    Didn't anybody love them
    like you love me
    'cause that's all they need.

• • •

## Janis Ian

Janis Ian is an international recording star and hit songwriter. Among her many hits are "Society's Child," "At Seventeen" and "Jesse." Her songs have been recorded by such artists as Bette Midler, Glen Campbell, Cher, Amy Grant, Joan Baez, Mel Torme, Chet Atkins, Nana Mouskouri, Hugh Masekela, Diane Schuur and Etta James. She has won two Grammy awards, has been honored by the National Association of Songwriters, has written music for several feature films and two television movies-of-the-week, and has garnered eighteen gold and seventeen platinum LPs worldwide.

# Making Demos

## JOHN BARILLA

Songwriters need to have a good-sounding representation of their songs in order to market them. Gone are the days of personal auditions—where writers would sit down at a piano or strum a guitar and perform their songs for the publisher. Today we live in a high-pressure, high-tech world where the scarcest commodity is time. A publisher simply does not have time to give each aspiring songwriter a personal interview. Instead the preferred currency is the demo tape.

The demo tape is convenient for many reasons. One is that it gives the publisher a chance to audition a song several times: in the office, in the car, on the home stereo; or to pass it to a colleague for a second opinion. This gives them a chance to listen more objectively to the songs in a relaxed atmosphere. Second, it gives the publisher a way of gauging how the song might sound as a final product. This is, of course, the reason why a songwriter needs to have the highest quality demo possible. Because of the technological age we live in, every musical product can very quickly be compared to another. The result is that the level of expectation that publishers have today is far greater than it was only a few years ago.

This does not mean that your demo has to have all the polish of a commercial record, nor should you need to "get yourself in hock" to finance it. In fact, most publishers agree they don't want to hear an "ultraslick" production, because it actually limits their ability to "color" the sonic picture the way they want to. On the other hand, the totally "bare bones" demo (e.g., guitar and vocal) is usually not sufficient either. The ideal demo is really somewhere in between.

What are the characteristics of a good demo?

First of all, a good demo has to be well recorded. A noisy or distorted tape will never do. In the age of the compact disc (CD)—whose sound is virtually noise-free—music industry professionals have gotten used to clean, clear-sounding recordings. We can never turn back the clock here, nor should we want to. The technology to make excellent-sounding tapes is commonly available. Songwriters simply need to learn to use it or work with someone who does.

Another point here is musicianship. You don't have to be a great musician to make your own demos, but you have to be able to play the parts you design accurately and confidently. It probably sounds too obvious to mention, but making sure every instrument is *completely* in tune with the others is something that is frequently overlooked. So is the matter of timing—how consistently the various parts and rhythms work together. Once again, the perception of these things in the ears of the listener has gotten much more critical today. Why? Simply because of the impact of computer technology on music. Most pop records are at least partially played by computer. (Not that the computer does it all by itself, of course. It needs to be programmed by a musician. But once it has been programmed, it is capable of executing its parts flawlessly: perfect tuning, perfect timing.) Fortunately, or unfortunately as the case may be, a live musical performance will automatically be judged by the standards of a computer performance, so musicianship needs to be accurate in every way.

Finally, we must consider the matter of

arrangement and production. Poor judgment in these areas can kill even a very good song. You can compare it to a woman who wears an evening gown to an afternoon picnic. It will be grossly out of place and draw undue attention to itself. So what if you have this incredible smokin' guitar solo on your tape, but the lyrics are buried beneath the music? Get the picture? What the songwriter needs to constantly keep in mind is that the arrangement and production should not get in the way of the song. Instead, they should draw the listener into the song the way a picture frame helps focus attention on the picture. (We will discuss these matters in more detail in the section entitled "Planning Your Production.")

So if you are just getting started in songwriting or are already experienced at the craft, read on. There will be many helpful tips for the novice and journeyman alike!

## Getting Started

A songwriter can record a demo in two basic ways: You can have an experienced person produce your demo for you, or you can do it yourself. Most songwriters eventually learn to produce demos on their own — even if they don't play any of the instruments. Today, you cannot write songs without being a bit of a producer at heart. Every genre of music will have its own pet sounds, and songs are quite often built integrally around these sounds. For example, it would be difficult to imagine a reggae tune without a heavy bass line, or a heavy metal tune without a screaming guitar. So before you even get started writing your song, you make certain production decisions. In a sense, you are already "producing" your demo as you write your song.

Nonetheless, since there are only a few ways to make a successful production and literally hundreds of ways to blow it, you may be wise to get a more experienced hand to help you on your initial recording sessions. Local recording studios often know or have on staff musically experienced people who specialize in helping songwriters put together professional-sounding demos. Very often these producers will offer you a "package deal": For a fixed fee they will guarantee you a final product — no matter how long it takes to complete. To find such a producer is easier than it might seem. You might want to start by shopping around for studios that specialize in songwriter demos. These are probably not going to be the glitzy, upscale, state-of-the-art-type studios. (You actually want to stay away from them, because their rates will probably be much higher than you would care to pay for a demo.) Typically, you will find yourself in a small, unimposing studio (typically an eight-track facility), perhaps even in someone's house or apartment. These humble home facilities, which have been dubbed "electronic cottages," are turning out a vast majority of the demos on the market. Whatever the facility, remember these two points: *Shop wisely*. Any people who purport to produce songs for other people should be able to play a demo of their work for you. If you have any doubts about their ability or if they seem to be unable to adapt to your style of music, then keep on looking. *Negotiate*. On the other hand, if the producer seems like a good candidate, negotiate in earnest. *Everything* is negotiable in this business. The best deal, of course, is a "win-win" situation; both parties are satisfied that they are not being exploited.

Another approach to demo-making is organizing it yourself in a larger, commercial recording studio where you simply pay for the time you use by the hour. If you have a band already in place or at least an "ad hoc" group of musicians who are committed to rehearsing and helping you record in a professional studio, this is definitely the way to go. Most of your "trial and error" solutions will have been worked out in rehearsal before you walk into the studio. If you are happy with the way the band plays your song, all it will take is a competent recording engineer to capture it on tape. It's really a nice way to record if you can do it. It's cost effective, and provided the musicians are all competent players, the demo should have a nice, natural kind of feel to it. Unfortunately, most people have difficulty in dedicating their time to an unpaid, speculative project, and it is not an easy task to keep a band together. In fact, for most songwriters it is a luxury they may never experience.

For most songwriters, it's more practical to go with electronic music production. After all, drum computers never slow down or speed up unless you tell them to, they never show up late for rehearsal, they remember their parts perfectly and they never have bad attitudes or grumble about going over the same song incessantly. They are humble servants, albeit a little mechanical, but they are not subject to the shortcomings of human personality. They will get the job done. It is no doubt easy to see why a majority of demo productions are done with synthesizers (electronic keyboards), sequencers (programmed performances), and drum computers. Add to this a live guitar and some vocals, and you can have a dynamite demo without dealing with personality hassles.

## Setting Up a Home Studio

You can hire somebody to do electronic production for you, or better yet, you can put that money towards your own "electronic cottage." More and more songwriters today are opting for recording themselves in their own home simply because in the long run it is *much* more cost-effective to do this. Certainly, there are many valid reasons why songwriters might want to pay a professional producer to record their songs, but if you have a serious commitment to writing songs, putting together your own "electronic cottage" is *definitely* the way to go. Even if you are not the hottest musician, as long as you can conceptualize your ideas, you can utilize this marvelous technology to "iron out the wrinkles." In your own studio you will be able to do it over and over again — without being held to the tyranny of the clock (hourly rates in recording studios) or feeling like your musicianship is being judged by another per-

son. In the end, simply having the liberty to fiddle with a tune until you are happy with it will ultimately result in a very satisfactory product.

And if you ask your accountant, you will certainly find out that purchasing equipment — hardware — is a much sounder investment than paying for intangible production services on your songs. Amortizing your equipment over several years, you will find that the break-even point comes rather quickly for an active songwriter. In other words, you could pay for your entire home studio for what it might cost you to do several songs with a professional producer. The benefits also include having an opportunity to beef up your own musicianship and ultimately having equity in your equipment. And if you should ever want to sell or trade up equipment, used recording equipment retains much of its value. Likewise (depending on how you set up your tax returns), there may be some legitimate tax write-offs for these capital investments. The list of advantages to doing it yourself is really quite extensive.

### Outfitting a home studio
If you have decided to make the plunge and put together your own facility, there are a few things you should keep in mind. First, decide on what you can afford to spend. Your budget can be small or large; it makes no difference. At any budgetary level, it is possible to buy a piece of equipment that will definitely improve your songwriting. You don't need every gadget in the store. Just buy what you can reasonably afford, knowing that later you can always add to it.

The most basic piece of equipment you will need is a multi-track tape recorder. (It's called multi-track because it allows instruments to be recorded synchronously, one track at a time.) While you may want or be able to afford a more elaborate setup, the four-track recorder has really become a staple with songwriters. Many manufacturers put out versions of four-track recorders. They are usually small, portable, self-contained units that allow you to record, mix and put various effects on the tracks. Some models have built-in echo or reverb, but all of them will allow you to plug in other gear to give you various sound effects. (Good quality four-track recorders can be purchased for as low as $400.)

You can simply plug a microphone, guitar or electronic keyboard directly into your four-track and start recording. But if you want to get that smooth, professional sound on your final mix (the final blend of all the recorded tracks with effects), a good-quality reverb is almost imperative. Fortunately, technology is on our side here. Due to recent advances in electronics, the prices for quality audio equipment have fallen sharply. An excellent digital reverb unit can be purchased for as low as $100. More versatile units that do other effects (as well as reverb) are somewhat more expensive, but still quite reasonably priced.

There are, of course, lots of toys to choose from — the possibilities are virtually endless. But to make basic recordings — to play your instruments and sing along with yourself — the above mentioned setup will get you rolling for around $600.

The next stage in extending a simple setup like this is to add some MIDI equipment. (In case you don't know, MIDI stands for *musical instrument digital interface*. It is simply a standard for communication between special-purpose computers that allows the various units to operate synchronously with one another.) Devices that can be operated through MIDI are virtually all electronic keyboards, drum computers (which contain digitally recorded "real" drums) and of course, sequencers (computers that memorize performances played on MIDI instruments and allow you to edit the performance and play it back later). James Becher's tape and text on "Understanding MIDI," which are included in this series, will provide a more thorough background on these useful devices. For now, let it suffice to say that the acquisition of a sequencer, drum computer and at least one synthesizer will greatly expand the potential of the simple four-track studio.

Since MIDI equipment can operate in tandem (synchronously) with your tape recorder, the number of sounds you can use in your production now is no longer limited by the number of tracks on your tape machine!

The point here is simple. You can start out with very basic equipment and, without ever outgrowing it, gradually expand until you have everything you need to make professional-sounding demos.

## Basics of Multi-Track Recording

Whether you record at home or in a studio, you should be familiar with the basic equipment used for recording and devices for manipulating sound. Manipulating sound is covered in the section called "A Guide to Signal Processing" (page 34) and on the accompanying tape. Here's an overview of the equipment you'll use.

### Tape recorders and mixers

Songwriters will need a multi-track recorder (such as the four-track mentioned earlier). Four-track recorders usually use standard cassette tapes. If you want more tracks there are models of multi-track recorders featuring six, eight, twelve, or sixteen tracks. Some use cassettes, but some utilize ¼″ or ½″ reel-to-reel tape.

You'll also need a stereo cassette machine for mixdown. You'll take your four, eight or sixteen tracks of recorded sounds and mix them together in varying proportions with some added effects, and the final stereo mix will then be permanently recorded on the stereo cassette machine. No matter how many separate tracks you have recorded, no matter now many effects you add, the end product is ultimately reduced to two tracks — that is, stereo (see figure 1).

If you use this kind of setup, remember this: Always use the highest quality cassette tape possible (either high-bias chrome or metal) when recording your multi-track tape or your mix-down. Also, use noise-reduction (Dolby or dbx) whenever possible, because this will result in a quieter,

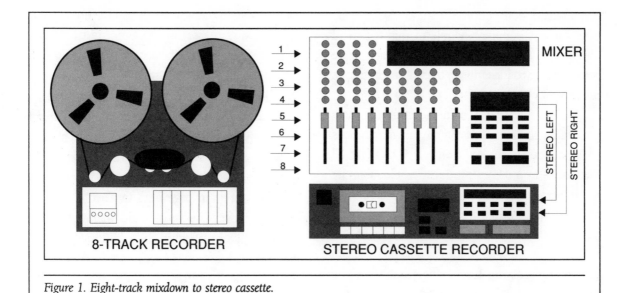

*Figure 1. Eight-track mixdown to stereo cassette.*

more professional-sounding product. Likewise, remember to clean the tape heads with an approved head-cleaning solvent. Also, don't forget to demagnetize the heads periodically. (The heads retain extra magnetism, which can cause noise and distortion on tape. Demagnetizers are available at stereo shops and electronics stores.)

For a more flexible setup, you might consider buying a mixer and tape recorder as separate units. In this way you can find the mixer that has more of the features you want and match it with a tape recorder of your preference. This custom approach is generally favored by more experienced songwriters, but first-time users generally are more comfortable with a combination unit.

### Wiring

Songwriters, in their zeal to be creative, often connect their recording equipment together in a very haphazard way. They often think, "What's the big deal, you just hook it up, right?" Well, yes and no. Remember that a chain is only as strong as its weakest link. And a little, "insignificant" item like the connecting wires can seriously degrade the sound of your studio. Fortunately, a few simple, commonsense rules will keep you on the straight and narrow path.

1. Use high-quality cable. If you've invested several hundreds of dollars in equipment, don't skimp here! High-quality cable contains metal plugs on both ends and has rugged metal "shielding" inside the wire. This shielding will help ward off outside interference which may affect the quality of the sound.

2. Use cables of appropriate length — not longer than necessary. The longer the length, the greater the opportunity for noise to enter into your system.

3. Never run audio cables parallel to power cables. If you do, hum might be induced into your sound. If audio cables and power cables cross, let them do so (whenever possible) at right angles. Doing this will neutralize the deleterious effect of the magnetism that is emitted from the power cables.

## Pre-Production Planning

Getting started is always the most difficult part of any demo production. Whether you are working with a four-track or a sixteen-track recorder, the dilemma is always the same: Where do I begin? While there can be no neat answer to this question, some guidelines may be helpful.

First of all, what kind of song is it? What genre of music does it represent? Unless it is a totally novel piece of music, chances are the listener (especially a publisher) will hear it with certain musical conventions in mind. It's usually best not to disappoint people in this regard. If the song you are about to demo purports to be contemporary dance music, then it had better be rhythmically exciting.

Whatever the style, plan to feature the most prominent element of that genre as a major focus of your production. You don't need to fill in all the blanks as a record producer would. You are making a sketch. A sketch can imply the whole aspect simply by drawing on the most prominent feature of the subject. Ever see a caricature of Bob Hope? His unmistakable jut-jaw and ski-nose can be represented with just a single line. It is the same with music. Display the dominant element of the musical form and you have successfully identified it. While this kind of focus and self-restraint is always the hallmark of good production, it is particularly important in demo production. Leave something to the imagination!

### Structuring your song

Plan your structure carefully. By this we mean the length of the song, the number of measures allocated to the verse, chorus, bridge, etc., and the overall order that you give to a song.

First of all, each song needs to have a "hook." A hook can be defined as a single, memorable idea that is repeated several times throughout the song. Usually, it contains the title of the song, but sometimes it may not. It can even be an instrumental line. In any case, a hook serves to identify the song and help the listener retain it in memory. In commercial writing, the stronger the hook the better. Publishers are well-schooled in the art and science of communication—not because they all have Ph.D.'s, but because experientially they have learned what motivates the person on the street.

Let your arrangement, then, support the hook. If the hook occurs at the beginning of a chorus, let the preceding section (usually a verse) direct attention toward the hook. One way to do that is by a dynamic buildup (a "power chord"

on a rock-style guitar or a "fill" on the drum part). Another way to set up the hook is by silence (stopping the music a beat or two before so that the hook will enter by surprise).

Also, remember to "block-out" your tune. In other words, divide it into sectional blocks and test out various combinations of those blocks. Just as a graphic artist might take various blocks (pictures, headlines, text, etc.) and move them around on a given page until the layout is maximally effective, you too should manipulate the building blocks of your composition until you have ordered it for maximum impact. While your song may have a certain natural structure to it in its raw form, very often it pays to restructure it, putting the most memorable element first, to attract and hold the listener's attention.

Learn to recognize and label all sections of your song. Below is a list of some conventional definitions for pop music. While most songs will contain only a few of these blocks, eventually you will find a use for all of them. At right is a lyric sheet for the song on the accompanying tape. Each of its structural parts is labeled.

1. *The Chorus*—the section of the song that is most often repeated. Lyrically, it generally contains a summation or conclusion that is often a response to the problem set forth in the verse.

2. *The Verse*—the section of the song that tells the story. The full development of the narrative usually occurs over the course of two or three verses that are separated by choruses.

3. *The Bridge*—the one section of the tune that is usually never repeated. It is designed to serve as a release or diversion from the tensions set up by the cycle of verse/chorus. Lyrically, it usually offers an additional insight not found in the body of the song. Musically, bridges are typically *unrelated* to the rest of the song in terms of chords. An effective bridge provides a little "dash of salt" which momentarily takes the listener away from the song, and then affords him comfort when the song returns to its normal pattern.

# The Closest Thing To Love

Instrumental Intro:                                    (with drum and guitar
                                                        lick to set up verse)


Verse:        Had some business on Ninth Avenue         (guitar fill)
              Saw a couple—made me think of me and you  (guitar fill)
              Redheads still drive me crazy
              Can't believe they still faze me
              How come I never found someone new?       (drum fill to chorus)


Chorus:       You were the closest thing to love        (3-part harmony)
              The closest thing to love I've ever known
              You were the closest thing to love
              The closest thing to love I've ever known


Verse:        I know this ain't no perfect world        (guitar fill)
              and I'm not lookin' for a perfect girl    (guitar fill)
              Why are all the good ones taken
              Gettin' tired of all this fakin'
              I'm just lookin' for one real pearl        (drum fill to chorus)


Chorus:       'Cause baby . . .                         (3-part harmony with
              You were the closest thing to love        small variation on lead
              The closest thing to love I've ever known vocal)
              You were the closest thing to love
              The closest thing to love I've ever known


Bridge:       I keep my heart undercover                (guitar and piano fills)
              Your memory's like a tattoo
              How can I find another lover
              When I compare them all to you?


Chorus:       You were the closest thing to love        (3-part harmony
              The closest thing to love I've ever known repeating with "gospel
              You were the closest thing to love        style" improvisation on
              The closest thing to love I've ever known lead vocal)
                                                        (fade out)

4. *The Intro* — simply a short (usually musical, but occasionally lyrical) section that eases the listener into the song. An example would be a short taste of the chorus or verse played instrumentally before the first verse is sung.

5. *The Outro* — a musical figure that ends a song rather than begins it.

6. *The Tag* — pertains to the end of the song, but usually implies a variation on the chorus that has been modified to repeat over and over again.

7. *The Interlude* — usually a short, add-on instrumental section designed to prevent the main sections of a song from running into each other too quickly. It's something like an intro, but occurs internally rather than in front of the song. It is commonly used to separate verses in songs that cycle through two verses before clobbering the listener with the chorus. Such a technique maintains the tension set up by the verses much longer, thereby magnifying the hook when it finally occurs.

8. *The Pre-Chorus* — a term used to describe a short section of the tune that functions distinctly from the verses, but is required to precede the chorus. As such, it acts as a connective between verse and chorus.

You may be able to define other blocks according to the style of your music. Once having blocked out your song so that it holds your interest, you should time it to see that it is not too long for the kind of song you are writing. Pop songs are usually between three and four minutes long. Dance tunes, of course, can be somewhat longer.

## Orchestration

Orchestration involves deciding what instrument will play what parts. Once the structure has been laid, it is then time to "fill in the colors." I think in this regard it is very fortunate that most songwriters have limited resources. If they had access to every instrument they could fancy and unlimited tracks to record them on, they would waste a lot of time and come up with extremely cluttered demos.

There is a certain liberation in having only four or eight tracks to record on. A lot of goofy detours are impossible. You will have to "go for the jugular vein" of your listener by including only the impactful parts. This does not mean that your demos should ever be bland and predictable. On the contrary, because you have fewer options you need to be craftier than the self-indulgent record producer who can record dozens of tracks from which he will later select only a few. In a sense, having fewer instruments and fewer tracks can really help you focus your production in a very effective way.

You must simply list your priorities — what style of music, who your audience is, what instruments are characteristic of that style — and make sure that you feature the most important elements (bass and drums in a dance tune, guitar in a rock tune, etc.). You will have to figure out how to best allocate the tracks available to you. As we will discuss in the following section, there are ways to consolidate tracks — so that two or more previously recorded tracks are merged on a new track, thereby freeing some tracks for additional recording. But all this requires planning. You will learn how best to maximize the available resources simply by doing it, making mistakes, and retrospectively figuring out a better way. It's sort of like playing checkers or tic-tac-toe. You need to observe the current situation, anticipate possible moves, and exercise your options based on previous planning. It's always good to model these things with pencil, paper and a large eraser. It's better to erase these theoretical strategies on paper than to find yourself boxed into a corner later!

## Recording Your Demo

Once you've decided on an arrangement for your song and which instruments will be playing on your basic tracks, it's time to get it on tape. If you are oriented towards live playing, and you are a versatile musician, you will probably be laying down each track—one track at a time. If your song has been written on guitar or keyboard, you will either "mic-up" (set a microphone in front of) the guitar or keyboard, or if they are electric or electronic instruments, you will simply take a wire and plug it in directly. In either case, it's good to hear some steady rhythm from a drum computer or metronome while recording, just to help you keep your beat. If you have a drum part already worked out, you can record that first and play along with it on guitar or keyboard.

### Basic tracks

The guitar or keyboard is the basic accompaniment instrument. (If you had to play the song solo at some concert and you could only choose one instrument to accompany you, it would certainly not be a bass or a drum, but most likely a keyboard or guitar). This is true for most kinds of pop music, but for dance music or rap music, bass and drums may be virtually the only instruments in the production. The point is this: Always record the most centrally important instruments—the basic tracks—first.

Many songwriters today prefer a more "electronic" approach to recording their demos. Rather then actually playing the parts into a tape recorder, they program the parts in a MIDI sequencer. While a certain amount of actual playing still goes on, the MIDI sequencer will memorize the performance—mistakes and all—and the programmer will then be able to go back and methodically edit the mistakes until the performance is perfect. Since these devices can "auto-correct" certain timing errors in the performance, and can also record at super-slow speeds without affecting the pitch (as a normal tape recorder would), the programmer can get a near perfect performance happening in the sequencer *prior to* recording it on tape. That being done, the songwriter can just push the button on the sequencer and allow the sequencer to "play" whatever instruments are attached to it through MIDI. He can then rather passively record this performance on his multi-

track. As you can see, this method has a lot of possibilities, particularly for the marginal musician. There are a lot of variations on the MIDI production method, which are covered in depth in Jim Becher's section entitled, "Understanding MIDI."

For our purposes though, all we really need to be concerned with is that—whether "live" or through MIDI—your basic tracks are recorded first. The term "basic tracks" does not invariably refer to the same parts but rather implies recording the harmonic and rhythmic "foundation" for the song. It sets the stage for the entire production.

When recording basic tracks—or, for that matter, any tracks—setting the record level is really a critical operation. The "0" marking on the VU meter (see figure 3) is certainly a good guideline, but to really optimize your recording, some experimentation is in order. For very clangorous sounds—like a cymbal or tambourine—"0 VU" may actually be too much. In these cases, the sound is so sharp that the meter is not fast enough to catch it. It says "0," but it really is higher. If it's too high, it will cause "distortion" on your tape—a truly hideous sound! On the other hand, if you decide to play it safe and record everything below "0 VU," what you may find is that your tape has become inordinately noisy. Why? Because tape itself generates a certain amount of noise. When the meaningful sound on tape is sufficiently loud, the noise becomes insignificant by comparison. When the sound on tape is weak, the noise then

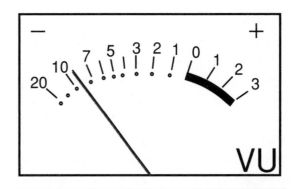

*Figure 3. Typical VU meter.*

becomes an audible factor. There is not a lot of leeway. To get an excellent recording you have to tread the fine line between noise and distortion. Since for each type of instrument—voices included—optimum practical recording levels may differ, it is good to experiment until you find out what works best with your system.

## Overdubs

Overdubs—the process of adding tracks one at a time—may include vocals (both lead and background) and any other instruments beyond the basic rhythm section that will give some additional flavor to the track. It is not surprising that these flavor-enhancing tracks are sometimes referred to as "sweeteners." When recording overdubs, the musician will listen to previously recorded tracks through headphones and add another track to what has already been recorded. This process can go on and on until you run out of tracks.

But what do you do when you are down to your last track and still have two more parts to record? There are really two ways to deal with this: You could have two musicians (or a MIDI sequencer) play the two parts at the same time and record them on one track. That concept is called "busing" or pre-mixing. The other concept is called "bouncing." It really means that two or more previously recorded tracks can be mixed together and re-recorded on another track. Once the bounce has been successfully done, you can then use this consolidated track in place of the originals. The two, three or more original tracks are no longer necessary and are therefore available to record on again.

If you bounce carefully—by planning it in advance—you can get some pretty good mileage out of even a four-track recorder. Extensive bouncing, however, can be tricky. For one thing, it's really not good to bounce to adjacent tracks. In other words, if you had tracks one and two recorded on and you wanted to bounce them (on a four-track recorder), you would do well to avoid

bouncing to track three. (In a pinch it's possible to do it, but the sound quality will suffer.) If, however, you bounced to track four you would preserve the quality of the tracks fairly well. I say fairly well, because technically the transfer is not 100 percent efficient. A little noise is added each time you bounce, and if you bounce the same tracks enough times (i.e., if you bounce the bounce, then bounce the bounce of the bounce, etc.), you will eventually hear a noticeable degradation of the sound. So it's best not to get too carried away.

Another tough reality of bouncing is that once the original tracks have been merged onto the bounce track, they can never be separated. That's obvious. But what may not be so obvious is that the relationship (relative loudness) of the permanently joined tracks is fixed. So you simply must learn to "hear" *in advance* what it will sound like in the final mix—*before* you bounce. This really calls for an intelligent estimate. After a time (and a few mistakes), you will get good at it and bouncing will be a valuable technique to expand the capabilities of your multi-track recorder.

One thing that will help make a bounce go smoother is to choose compatible instruments for the bounce. For example, bass and drums would be a good combo. You can usually mix them in about equal proportions and be fairly certain that they will work quite well in the final mix. An example of a bad combo would be lead vocal and drums. What if the drums turned out to overpower the vocal? You would be in a tough spot!

The other downside to bouncing is that when two or more tracks are joined as one, you cannot separate them later on during the mix. They will have to be placed in the center of the mix, rather than left or right. This sounds like a limitation, but it can actually be a blessing. First of all, mixing in monaural is easier. There are fewer things to mess up. Second, monaural sound is powerful and sounds good even if it's played on a trashy stereo. (Most radio and TV commercials—where impact has to be maximized—are mixed in mono.) So in a sense, a monaural mix is virtually idiot-proof! You probably would not release a record in monaural today, but for demos it's just fine.

## Mixing Your Demo

Mixing is a critical aspect in the process of making a demo. The power of your lyrics and the care you put into recording can sometimes go unnoticed because of a bad mix. Do you know what the primary cause of a bad mix is? It's not knowing when to stop! This problem is not limited just to songwriters. Even professional mixers have to exercise self-control in this area.

You can probably relate to this scenario: You've been working on a song, off and on now, for several weeks. After each session you do a rough mix just for kicks. The mixes always seem to have a nice "feel" to them. Then one day you decide that you've finished laying down tracks. It's time for a final mix. You are excited. You want the final mix to be perfect. You've got lots of ideas on how you will treat the various tracks. You say to yourself, "If the rough mixes sounded so good, imagine how good the final mix will be." You work hard at the mix. Hours pass. It's still not right. You make some more adjustments. It's getting better. No, it's still not right. Finally, in weariness you say, "Well, maybe my ears are deceiving me. This is the best I can do. Perhaps it will sound okay tomorrow morning." In the morning you listen to it. Lo and behold it does sound pretty good, better than you imagined it would. But just out of curiosity you listen to a tape of one of your rough mixes, and the spontaneity and freshness of the rough mix really blows you away. By comparison, the final mix sounds polished but stale. You conclude that somewhere in the process you've lost the source of your initial inspiration. Why does this happen, and how can you avoid it?

The main reason mixes sometimes are unsatisfactory is that the mixer loses sight of priorities. By keeping these things in mind you can avoid the trap of overmixing and come up with professionally acceptable mixes every time. Here are some priorities you might want to keep in mind.

1. You are mixing a demo, not a record. Unlike a record producer, your reputation will not rise and fall on the cleverness of your mix. An overly produced mix will hurt your chances of getting a song covered because it will draw more attention to the production than to the song. The rule is Keep it simple!

2. Remember your priorities. This will always help you to keep the mix in focus. Pop songs always feature vocals. The lyrical content is definitely of interest to your publisher, and he is not interested in wasting time trying to decipher them from your demo. Even in rock tunes which feature powerful guitar parts, the lyrics must always be audible. Other musical elements essential to the style of the music should get the next priority (whether it be guitar on rock tunes, drums on dance music, or bass on ballads). Then the remaining tracks should be brought up in the mix to the point where they are most effective. But never allow them to override the vocals or dominant instruments.

3. Check the sonic balance. In other words, does the mix contain sufficient brilliance in the high frequency range, strong (but not harsh) mid-range sounds, and a rich warmth in the low end (bass range)? A mix really needs to have good representation in all three areas. Without balance here, it will ultimately receive a lukewarm response. Why? Because without a sensible ratio of high, mid and low frequencies, the mix will not bear repeated listenings. It will unconsciously grate on people's nerves and they will tire of it. An effective demo must be pleasant sounding. That's the bottom line. While excessive highs will titillate the senses initially, soon thereafter the senses will become saturated. Such a mix, though apparently "hot" will also sound thin and shrill on certain systems and make tape duplication more difficult. It's not worth the thrill! The same with too much bass. Bass frequencies are big fat ones. They move a lot of air, take up a lot of space on your tape. While people do respond viscerally

to bass (and this of course is good), an excess will literally squeeze out the audibility of the other sounds. If you have a tape with too much bass, remove some of the bass with an equalizer or the tone controls on your stereo and see how the vocal begins to be more audible. You didn't boost the vocal here, you just removed the bass! To avoid this nasty phenomenon, always keep the idea of balance of in the forefront of your mind. (See figures 4 and 5 for samples of twelve-, eight- and four-track recording track sheets — the written records of how a multi-track tape is laid out.)

Using these three guidelines, you should be able to develop a method of mixing that will enable you to get a professional-sounding mix every time. See the next section, "A Guide to Signal Processing," to learn about using equalizers, reverb, delay, compression and other types of processing to help you shape the sound of the final mix. The single most important parameter of a mix, however, is simply the relative loudness of each of the tracks. If you keep your priorities straight, seek sonic balance, and remember that you are mixing a demo not a record, your mix will always showcase your songwriting in the proper light.

## A Guide to Signal Processing

The following is a brief introduction to some of the most popular sound processing devices used in recording today. Used properly, they will help your demo mixes sound more polished and professional.

### Equalizers

Equalizers (see figure 6) are a very important feature of any mixer. Essentially, they are just sophisticated tone controls and their purpose is just what the name implies — they are used to bring equality to the sound in terms of high, mid and low frequency ranges. The equalizer is perhaps the single most valuable tool in the arsenal of sound-manipulating devices. Equalization, however, is an art. And it can only be learned by doing

it. Properly used, the equalizer can do some marvelous things to the sound quality. It can add a brilliance and shimmer to vocals, alleviate harshness in certain sounds, and give you bass that you can actually feel. When you get your hands on one, be sure to do a lot of experimentation. It will pay off in the long run.

### Reverb

While reverb is still (and probably will always be) the single most important effect used in recordings, there are only a few units on the market that do "reverb only." A few years ago, a reverb was a reverb, a delay was a delay, etc. But due to the recent incredible advances in electronic technology, it is now possible to have one unit perform several functions simultaneously. So you may go to a music store to buy a reverb and come home with something that does reverb and a whole lot more!

In any case, reverb is still applied to the mix as reverb, no matter what kind of package it may come in. What is reverb? It is simply the sum total of all the reflections of a sound bouncing off of the walls around it. Like singing in the shower, for example. Everyone likes to do that because the reverb from the highly reflective tile surfaces is pretty flattering. Go into a bigger bathroom — like the one in your high school gym, and the reverb will sound more intense because the walls are further apart. Therefore the reverb takes longer to die down. The time it takes for reverb to die down after the actual sound has stopped is called its "decay time" (see figure 7). Take it one step further, and you are in a large cathedral or perhaps the famous Taj Mahal in India. A building of this size builds up tremendous amounts of reverb! Get the picture?

What modern digital reverbs do is to simulate by way of mathematics the important sonic characteristics of various rooms. It's what you would call a computer model. (A well-known computer model can be found in the "flight simulator" programs now available for home computers. Origi-

**Title:** The Closest Thing to Love

| 1 | 2 | 3 | 4 | 5 | 6 |
|---|---|---|---|---|---|
| Bass | Background Vocals (L) | Guitar #2 (heavy sound) | Keyboard Mix (L) | Lead Vocals | Keyboard Mix (R) |

| 7 | 8 | 9 | 10 | 11 | 12 |
|---|---|---|---|---|---|
| Drums (L) | Drums (R) | Guitar #1 Bright (L) | Guitar #1 Bright (R) | Background Vocals (R) | Keyboard Pad |

*Figure 4. Above is the track sheet for the song on the tape accompanying "Making Demos." Let's analyze it and answer some obvious questions: 1. The designations L and R mean that during the mix, there are channels "placed" on the left side or right side of the mix—emanating primarily from that speaker. Four-track studios don't do too much with this concept, called "stereo panning," but eight-, twelve-track and larger studios frequently record two tracks of the same instrument so they can spread them apart during the mix, making the sound more spacious. 2. While the tracks might seem as if they're not in a neat sequential order (e.g. background vocals are on track two and track eleven), there is a method to the madness. Many of these tracks are "composite tracks"—bounced from two or more other tracks that no longer exist. We needed to leave a space (some empty, non-adjacent tracks) in order to bounce them most efficiently. Here is where they ended up. 3. No matter how many tracks you start with, the final mixed product is two tracks (i.e., stereo).*

| 1 | 2 | 3 | 4 | 5 | 6 | 7 | 8 |
|---|---|---|---|---|---|---|---|
| Bass | Drums (L) | Drums (R) | Guitar Mix | Lead Vocal | Keyboard Mix | Background Vocals (L) | Background Vocals (R) |

| 1 | 2 | 3 | 4 |
|---|---|---|---|
| Bass and Drums | Lead Vocal | Keyboard | Guitar |

*Figure 5. With an eight-track recorder it's still possible (with careful planning of bounces) to maintain the "stereo-ization" of some tracks. Still, some small compromises must be made. On the twelve-track (see above), the two guitars were kept separate. Here they have been bounced down to one track. There was also no track available for the "pad" (a thick mush of synthesized textures used subtly to make the mix sound fuller), and the keyboards had to be reduced to one track instead of two. On a four-track recorder, everything is reduced to essentials. Bass and drums work well together on one track, with one track each for vocals and guitar. No stereo panning here, but the basic idea remains intact.*

nally designed to train pilots without actually putting them in the air, these programs give the participant a realistic flight experience while still on the ground.) You can learn a lot about sound just by fooling around with a digital reverb, but you really don't have to know a thing to use one. What is important is simply that you will have access to a lot of flattering acoustical environ-ments to sing in. From the bathroom to the Taj Mahal—and more!

### Delay

Have you ever shouted into a canyon? You say "Hello!" and then sometime later (depending on how deep the canyon is) you will hear "hello" again, but a little weaker than your original call.

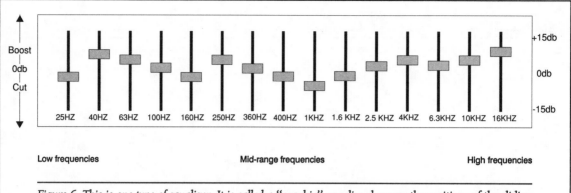

+15db
0db
-15db

Boost
0db
Cut

25HZ 40HZ 63HZ 100HZ 160HZ 250HZ 360HZ 400HZ 1KHZ 1.6 KHZ 2.5 KHZ 4KHZ 6.3KHZ 10KHZ 16KHZ

Low frequencies          Mid-range frequencies          High frequencies

*Figure 6. This is one type of equalizer. It is called a "graphic" equalizer because the positions of the sliding knobs on the front of the panel graphically illustrate which frequencies have been cut or boosted. The frequency spectrum runs from very low-pitched frequencies on the far left to very high-pitched frequencies on the far right. There are other types of equalizers, the main difference being that the better ones provide control over smaller, finer portions of the frequency spectrum.*

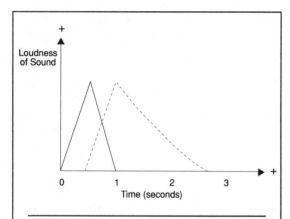

+
Loudness
of Sound

0    1    2    3    +
Time (seconds)

*Figure 7. Reverb decay time. The solid line depicts the original sound—for example, a cough in a gymnasium. The broken line indicates the reverb (sum of the echoes) as it builds up and then decays over time. Reverb time here is about 2.5 seconds.*

That "echo" then returns one or more times, successively weaker in volume until it runs out of energy and ceases. Well, this is precisely what goes on electronically in a device called a delay line. (A delay line may be packaged as a single "dedicated" unit or may be part of a "multi-effects processor" with other effects, like reverb, all in one box.)

Whatever sound you put into one of these gizmos is electronically shifted in time—delayed—so that the previously mentioned "can-

yon effect" is simulated. What's nice about doing it electronically is that you can actually change the size of the canyon. (Try doing that in the natural world!) Nonetheless, it is possible to get a delay so subtle that it appears to "fuse" with the original sound or so strident that it actually bounces along with the rhythm of the song. There are tons of interesting effects you can get from a simple delay line: echo, flanging, doubling, synchronous delays and many more. Sometimes these effects are sold as smaller specialized units—units that are more or less "tuned" to perform a specialized delay function. With most delay units, you should be able to derive any of these common effects. Let's look at some of them and how they might be used in the context of a demo production.

1. *Flanging* is achieved by using very small delay times and slightly varying the delay almost constantly. When I say small, I mean small! Like in the neighborhood of five ms (that's five milliseconds: five-thousandths of a second—or even less). This is admittedly a totally unnatural phenomenon. No canyon could be that small! It is totally electronic. But it's a very neat effect and works really well on stringed instruments. In excess, it will sound much like a jet on take-off (which could have certain applications). But used

subtly, it will impart a glistening, sweeping, shimmering kind of effect which, though hard to describe in words, is very easy to recognize. (For examples of all these effects, listen to Tape Two that accompanies this workbook.)

2. *Chorus* is related to flanging. It too utilizes a constantly varying short delay (but not as short as flanging). The effect seems to emulate the kinds of things that happen when a bunch of people sing or play the same part at the same time—a chorus or an ensemble. What happens in real life is that everybody tries his or her best to execute the part precisely. Nonetheless, there are certain natural differences. After all, "real" musicians (even excellently trained ones) are still human and imperfect. This human imperfection—being ever so slightly sharp or flat, early or late—is what gives the power and grandeur to a chorus. The differences are homogenized and the ear senses a larger-than-life corporate entity. Chorusing approximates this natural phenomenon. You can find many uses for chorusing, whether it be taking a single instrument making it sound like a section, or taking a section and making it sound larger still!

3. *Doubling* is simply another variation on the theme. If a delay line is set somewhere between twenty and sixty ms it will appear that an "alter-ego" of the original sound has formed. It's almost exactly like it, but ever so slightly (imperceptibly in some cases) behind, shadowing the original. Creating this sonic shadow gives the illusion of two voices or instruments doing the same part. It also has the effect of making a part sound fuller—"fatter," as producers would say—and making lyrics more intelligible to the listener.

4. *Slapback Echo*. Did you ever listen closely to old Elvis Presley records, Jerry Lee Lewis or an authentic rockabilly band? If you did, you most certainly heard slapback echo. Back in the 1950s, it was just about the only effect they had. Back then they did it all with tape recorders that were rigged to play a sound back a split second after it occurred. "Ka-chaa!" Something like a bullet ricocheting in a small concrete room. This gives a vocalist or guitarist a quick extra echo to his voice. For rather obvious reasons it is called a "slapback." Used subtly, it will liven up most any track. Used blatantly, it will give your song a distinct fifties flavor.

5. *Long Delays with Regeneration*. Well, it looks like we've come back to the canyon again. Remember the phenomenon we discussed about the echo repeating, but getting progressively weaker as it runs out of energy? Regeneration is that same phenomenon (an echo of an echo of an echo) performed electronically so as to control it. With the regeneration control, you can determine the number of echoes after the initial one.

There are lots of uses for this. A longer delay (which can be around 250 ms or as long as one or two full seconds) will give a vocal a smooth, ethereal quality, as if the singer were sitting atop a golden cloud. The extra echoes will serve to reinforce the lyrical ideas—particularly if the song is slow or has sparse lyrics. Another use is to increase the "flash" of a flashy guitar solo. Heavy metal guitarists love it. No matter how fast they play, it sounds as though they are playing much faster yet. The extra notes also seem to cover up a multitude of sins in terms of technique. A problematic note will just sail by in a flurry along with the host of good notes. The listener will never know the difference.

One additional use which has great application in dance music is the concept of "synchronous delay." The idea is to time out the echoes so that they bounce along with the rhythm of the music. In a sense, they then become another rhythm instrument, supporting the basic beat rather than being oblivious to it. This synchronous delay can be set by ear—experimentally twiddling the controls until the "bounce" is just right. Another way of accurately finding the delay setting(s) is to do it mathematically. It's very easy to do. Simply find out what the song's tempo is. You do this by sitting with a watch—like a doctor does when taking someone's pulse—and counting how many beats go by in the period of one minute. That is called the BPM (beats per minute) of the song. Next you simply take the BPM and divide it into 60,000 to get a useful delay setting. Say your song's tempo was 120 BPM. 60,000/120 = 500. So then, 500 ms is the basic setting for synchronous delay on that tune. Once you've derived the main setting (500 ms), you can also divide or multiply it by any small whole number (like two, three or four) to derive other musically useful settings.

### Dynamics controllers

There is a whole class of devices whose business is controlling the volume of a sound. Conceptually, I think it's useful to label these devices "dynamics controllers," but if you go out to buy one of these gadgets, you will have to call it by its traditional name: compressor, limiter, expander or gate. These units all control the relative loudness or softness of a sound but are used for different purposes.

A novice might ask this valid question: "If all these gadgets do is control loudness or softness of a sound, why can't I just manually reach over and twist the volume control—turn it up when I want it louder, down when I want it softer?" The answer is, of course you can! But you may not be able to do it as quickly and consistently as one of these devices. Besides that, you could turn into a nervous wreck trying to do that—if the song had a lot of volume changes. Your creative energy would be tied up doing a chore that a gadget can do much more efficiently. Enter compressors, limiters, expanders and gates.

Do you remember taking aptitude tests back in elementary school? They always had a section on analogies that had questions like this: "Up is to down as east is to _____?" If you answered "west," then you are capable of understanding how all these devices are related to each other. Get the picture? Compressor is to expander as limiter is to gate.

They do precisely what their names imply. A compressor smoothes out the sound so that loud passages are not quite so loud and soft passages—by comparison—are not quite so soft. An expander is simply the reverse side of the same coin: Louder sounds are stretched so as to be a little bit louder, and soft sounds—by comparison—appear softer yet. A limiter is related to the compressor in that it restricts the volume of a sound, but its method is a little different. A limiter simply sets a ceiling of loudness (a limit or threshold) beyond which the sound will be vigorously suppressed. The limiter says to the sound, "You are free to go up and down in loudness up to this point. But step over this line and you're gonna get squashed." The gate is analogous to a limiter in its methodology, but opposite in purpose. The gate says to the sound, "If you want to be heard, you simply must step over this line. If you don't, I will keep you silent." That's why it's often called a noise gate.

Some applications will probably be helpful here. Let's start with the gate. If, for example, we are recording a loud rock guitar, we might well record it through a gate. The reason is that in order to get the "heavy" guitar sound, the amplifier usually has to be overdriven—turned up to the point of distortion. A bad side effect of this is that when the guitar is not playing, the super-loud amplifier is putting out some very unflattering noise. You don't notice it when the guitarist is playing. But when he stops—even between short passages—it becomes annoying. The gate can fix that. The gate is set by the user so that when he plays, the gate "opens up," allowing sound to pass through. When he stops—even for just an instant—it shuts down, bringing precious silence to the guitar track.

The action of an expander is similar to that of the gate except it's not so radical. It's not all or nothing like a gate. Instead, it applies itself more gradually. Instead of totally shutting the gate, it will allow it to be partially open in varying degrees. Some sound will get through unhindered, some will be slightly suppressed, some very suppressed. The overall effect is to put more dynamics into something that might seem relatively monotonous. To kind of rephrase the popular saying, "It turns molehills into mountains." Every nuance becomes somewhat exaggerated. Want to get more "pop" out of a pickin' guitar part, more "snap" out of a snare drum? The expander may be the tool of choice.

The limiter, on the other hand, finds its usefulness when recording instruments that have too much "snap, pop, sizzle or boom." Such sudden bursts of loudness are sure to work havoc when you are trying to record them. Unless they are controlled—unless a limit is set for loudness—it will be quite difficult to get a clean, clear recording. For example, trumpets are known for their wide dynamic range. The natural "punch" of horns is why producers use them to add exclamation (!) to a soundtrack. But sometimes the blast of a trumpet can be excessive. The limiter simply helps keep this under control.

When a more gentle but constant massaging of the sound is needed, a compressor is generally used. Compressors can help smooth out the bumps in a performance by constricting the dynamics. This is particularly valuable in recording vocals. Singers are human. They are not always consistent in their loudness or their distance from the microphone. A vocal track with too many variations in volume may be difficult to mix with the rest of the music. Once it may appear too loud, another time it may become unintelligible—being swallowed up in the music. Applying a compressor to the vocal will even things out a bit, making its placement in the final mix much easier to determine.

To sum up this section, let it be said that it is not necessary to have all these various pieces of equipment in your home studio. Very decent-sounding demos can be made with only a four-track recorder and a microphone. But all of this stuff will make your life easier. Any of the above mentioned pieces—if used properly—will invariably help your recording sound more professional. With regard to compressors, limiters, expanders and gates, the songwriter will find that the trend among manufacturers today is to offer multipurpose dynamics processors that allow you to get any of the above functions from one unit. As you experiment and grow in your ability to produce demos, you will find these to be extremely helpful tools.

## Final Steps

Though you may have finished mixing, you are not finished with making a demo until you have packaged it for presentation. It may sound great in the studio, but it must also sound great in the office of your potential publisher. It is important that your cassette copies retain all the impact of your master tape. Unfortunately, this is not always the case. Many a good production has been marred by a lousy cassette copy. Truly, without proper care, much can get lost in the translation. So don't half-step the process here or your presentation will suffer.

If you are making a large demo run—say fifty or more copies, it may pay to have the copies done professionally. Professional duplication houses usually have all the tricks to making good copies. (Companies that offer so-called "real-time" duplication are usually the best, so shop around.)

But most songwriters will probably not be making such large runs. They will continue to make copies as they need them—maybe five or ten copies at a time. In that case, you need to know some of the tricks that the professional tape duplicators know.

First of all, use a good-quality cassette machine to make your copies. An inferior machine may add undue noise to your tape. If you don't own one, maybe you can borrow one for the day. You can also run two machines in tandem and make all your copies in half the time.

Second, use good-quality tape. Usually your machine has been adjusted at the factory for optimal performance on a certain brand of tape. You can quite often find out which tape the manufacturer recommends by looking at the specifications in the back of the user's manual or by calling the manufacturer. In most cases you should use that brand of tape. The machine will probably perform much better with the tape for which it has been calibrated. It's a good idea to experiment with a few brands of tape and see which one allows you to record the hottest, cleanest copies. In any case, don't skimp here. Use a good quality chrome ($CrO_2$) tape.

Noise reduction (Dolby or dbx) is nice for personal copies but unfortunately it hasn't met with universal acceptance throughout the industry. So when making copies to send out to publishers, most songwriters still opt for no noise reduction at all. To get a relatively noiseless tape copy without noise reduction, the copies have to be made very "hot"—that is, at the highest possible recording level. Of course they should not have any audible distortion, so you can't go too hot, but if you experiment you will be surprised how hot your tape copies can really get. Before making your copies, experiment a little bit to arrive at the optimum recording level. To do this you should simply record the loudest portion of your song on the cassette at a reasonable level and then record the passage repeatedly at progressively hotter levels (in say 1dB increments) until you have reached saturation (the point at which it begins to audibly distort). You may be shocked to see how high your meters read. If you just back the recording level off a little bit from this saturation level and record your song, you will undoubtedly have a clean, hot tape copy with relatively little noise even though you did not use noise reduction.

If you are recording a compilation of different songs on that tape, please remember that the recording level should be adjusted individually for each tune. You can't assume that the level for one song will work for the next one. If you don't make this test between each song you may find that there is a noticeable drop or rise in level between one song and another.

While it's important to find the optimal recording level for each song, it's also important to consider how the songs "mate-up" with each other. While a certain difference in level is normal—one song may end with a fade-out and the next start with a bang—you will want to order your songs so that they flow naturally from one to the next.

If you have access to two good-quality cassette machines, you can do a little "mastering" on your tape *before* making copies. In doing so you can bring a consistency to the songs that was not quite there before. Take your master tape and run it back through your mixing board (if you have a four-track mixer/recorder combination unit, you can use the mixer section for this purpose) before recording on the cassette machine. The cassette you derive from this process will not be for sending out to other people; it will be used to make the copies which you *will* send out. It is a one-of-a-kind compilation tape with however many songs you want on it, each recorded at the optimum level, in the appropriate order and with the proper spacing between them. Since this will be your personal "copy master," you will want to preserve the master quality as much as possible: Use metal tape and noice reduction (Dolby or dbx). In addition to matching recording levels, you will be able to do some of the neat tricks that mastering engineers do when they prepare a tape for mass duplication. Specifically, you can compensate for tonal imbalances by doing some subtle equalization. Sometimes relative to the other songs, a song may sound too dull or too bassy. Whatever they are, such deficiencies or excesses can easily be compensated with the equalizer on your console. It takes a little judgment to do this correctly, but after some practice you will find it to be an extremely valuable tool.

This "copy master" can now be used to make a large duplication run. All you have to do is plug the output of the one cassette machine into the other cassette machine, find a good average recording level and let the songs record. There is no longer any need to stop the tape between songs to make adjustments. Everything was done at the "mastering" stage. Now you can relax and make as many copies as you want without even thinking about it!

## Submitting Your Demos

Ideally, publishers say they like to hear from three to five songs on an *initial* demo tape. This gives them a chance to figure basically "where you're at" as a writer. Nonetheless, once you get to know a publisher, you can certainly send along just one or two tunes if you think the songs might interest that particular publisher.

Make sure your labels are clearly written. The stick-on labels that come with most commercial tapes are far too small to get enough information on them. You can, however, purchase full-size press-on labels (in almost any color you choose) from an audio supply house. If you use these quality labels, you will have room to type all vital statistics right on the cassette itself.

Make the entire presentation look attractive by including neatly typed lyric sheets (bearing the copyright notice on the bottom) and a thoughtfully written cover letter directed *specifically* to the publisher or record company you are pitching to (if possible, call ahead and get a name of someone to send it to, whom you inquire of later on). A nice touch is to put everything in a "pocket-binder" (folder) so that lyrics and letter do not get wrinkled. Insert the cassette tape in the pocket. If you are also marketing yourself as an artist, a "bio" (a narrative form of résumé) might also be included, along with a black-and-white photo, but for pitching songs this is overkill! Send it off in a padded mailing envelope. Keep a list of packages sent (to whom, date sent, response, etc.), and if you don't hear from them in three to four weeks, follow up with a phone call. Always be polite and respectful of their time. For more on pitching your demos, see Teri Muench's article, "The Art of Pitching Songs" (page 62).

Little things add up—all the way down the line. If you pay attention to the little things, the big things will take care of themselves. Good luck!

• • •

## John Barilla

John Barilla has been teaching people the art of recording for nearly a decade. A songwriter/ producer and recording engineer, he has been successful in distilling his experience into practical articles for *Mix*, *Electronic Musician* and several other magazines. Currently, he is senior editor for *db Magazine*, where his informative column, *Hot Tips for the Home Studio*, enjoys great popularity.

# Understanding MIDI

## JAMES BECHER

**M**IDI is a revolution in music-making for today's musicians and songwriters. MIDI allows a single person to play many instruments simultaneously, and the applications of this incredible music-making phenomenon are unending. The songwriter is bound only by the limits of his or her imagination in creating an entire electronic orchestra! With MIDI one person can be a duet or a full symphony orchestra. There is no longer a need to hire string or woodwind players, or even a drummer. One person can do it all. MIDI allows the songwriter to hear his or her musical composition fully orchestrated — instantly.

MIDI provides songwriters with the means of experimenting with many different sound colors, combining any number of individual sounds together to create interesting and complex textures that otherwise might not be possible to create in a nonelectronic, strictly acoustical environment. MIDI gives the songwriter whose playing abilities are short of virtuosity the chance to assemble a piece of music very slowly, and then speed it up to the desired tempo when the composition is fully completed. This technique of slowly building a musical composition is especially useful to the musically untrained songwriter because it encourages experimenting with various intervals and chords, and creates an immediate awareness of voicings.

Prior to MIDI, high-quality multilayer recording could only be done in an expensive recording studio, which usually involved many individuals, including musicians and engineers. When many people are involved in a recording project, other factors that affect the success of the project must

be considered. Effective communication with the musicians and engineers is absolutely essential. Individual temperaments and egos are also major factors in whether a recording session will go smoothly and productively or totally bomb, leaving the songwriter with a feeling of utter despair. Making music with MIDI, on the other hand, can be an absolute joy because every aspect of music composition and production is controlled by one person — the songwriter.

MIDI allows songwriters to challenge themselves constantly, and to build musical and production skills. MIDI encourages creativity and, more importantly, serves as a tool for virtually unlimited musical inspiration and spontaneity.

### What is MIDI?

MIDI is an acronym that stands for Musical Instrument Digital Interface. The best way to understand this highly technical-sounding concept is to break down the acronym and examine each of its component parts. I believe that we are all familiar with the idea of musical instruments and what they are, so I think that portion of the acronym speaks for itself. However, the musical instruments that MIDI refers to are electronic, not acoustic. We will be discussing electronic musical instruments that make use of MIDI, their variety and their applications shortly.

The next word in the acronym is "digital." Digital refers to information that is expressed in the form of a computer language that uses binary digits (0's and 1's) to form words known as digital words. The digital language is just like any other language, with one difference: Instead of using spoken words and letters to represent thoughts, digital language uses numbers to represent ideas and information. The word "interface" literally means an interaction between two or more systems. An interface is a direct connection or link between two or more electronic musical instruments, allowing information in the form of a computer language which uses binary digits to be transmitted and received back and forth between the various instruments. MIDI's digital interface allows electronic keyboards, drum machines, sequencers, personal computers, signal processors, etc., to be interconnected so that they may "communicate" or share digital information to form an efficient, cost-effective electronic orchestra. The idea of MIDI was conceived by five leading synthesizer (electronic keyboard) manufacturers, and is a successful attempt at achieving a truly universal interface for the diverse products offered by these electronic musical instrument manufacturers.

In order to understand MIDI, it may help to picture it as a communications system that allows different electronic musical instruments to "talk" to each other. All MIDI instruments can serve either as a transmitter, a receiver, or both. The types of information that are transmitted are "events" like key strokes, how hard a key was struck, how long the key was held down, when it was released, whether or not the sustain pedal (like that of a piano) was used, etc. There are many more unique types of digital information that can be transmitted as well, and they too will be explained shortly. These "events" are then converted into a binary code which is represented as digital information (computer language). This information is then sent or "transmitted" using a special connecting cable to the receiving electronic instrument(s). The "receiver" then decodes the digital information, sorting out the various commands sent, and performs the instructions sent to it from the transmitting instrument. The information sent from the transmitter to the receiver(s) is sent in a "serial" fash-

ion, that is, one bit of information at a time. Though this may sound like a slow process, it's not. MIDI information travels from the transmitting instrument to the receiving instrument at the incredible rate of approximately 32,000 bits of information per second!

MIDI's design provides for the transmission and reception of digital information between electronic musical instruments on sixteen "channels" simultaneously. This mode of simultaneous multi-channel reception is known in MIDI terms as the "omni" mode. "Omni" is latin for "all" (all sixteen channels). MIDI-equipped instruments also allow the user to select only one channel, of the sixteen available, that the instrument will receive on. When only one channel is selected, the MIDI instrument is said to be in the "poly" mode.

The transmission and reception of MIDI information is very much like that of television transmission and reception. The information — which, remember, is in the form of digital data — is transmitted from the source or "master" electronic instrument to the receiving electronic instrument(s) or "slave" as it is often called. This digital information may be transmitted on many or all of the sixteen channels available simultaneously. In this sense, the master instrument is acting like one or more television stations. The receiving instruments represent television sets with the ability to receive on all channels simultaneously. You can select which channel the receiving instrument(s) will "listen" to, in the same way you would use the channel selector on the television set to decide which program you want to watch. Just as several television sets could be hooked up to the same antenna, so could several MIDI-equipped electronic musical instruments be hooked up or "patched in" to the same musical source (the master instrument). The master sends an entire musical composition containing multiple channels of musical parts through a single MIDI cable to each slave, and in turn each slave is set to receive on its own independent channel of reception. This is how that electronic musical orchestra I spoke of is made possible, and I'll explain further.

All MIDI instruments have, as part of their architecture, special sockets or "ports" located on the rear panel. These ports use a European electrical connector known as a five-pin DIN connector. Most MIDI-equipped musical instruments have three ports, which are simply labeled MIDI-IN, MIDI-OUT and MIDI-THRU.

The MIDI-IN port does pretty much what it is labeled to do; it allows incoming digital information sent from the master—via a special MIDI cable—to enter into the instrument to then be deciphered, processed and executed.

The MIDI-OUT port is the point from which the series of instructions (key strokes, the length of time the keys were held down, sustain pedaling, etc.), now in computer language (digital form), are sent to the receiving MIDI instrument(s). These receiving instrument(s) accept the incoming data via the MIDI-IN jack located on the rear panel of the instrument(s). The master MIDI instrument is then not unlike a television station, or even a bunch of television stations, all situated within one central location, simultaneously sending their signals by way of a single DIN cable to a host of awaiting receiving instruments.

Before we continue, let's see what happens when only two MIDI instruments are connected together, which is really the most basic use of MIDI (see figure 1). By playing on the keyboard designated as the "master" keyboard (the MIDI cable is plugged into its MIDI-OUT port on the rear panel), we know that all of the information related to the performance (remember—keystrokes, note duration, use of the sustain pedal, etc.) is converted into digital data (computer language using 0's and 1's). It is then sent out or transmitted at an enormously fast rate—32,000 pieces of information per second, to the receiving electronic keyboard (the other end of the MIDI cable is plugged into its MIDI-IN port). The end result is this: Playing the notes on the first

## Make the Connection

A MIDI cord is plugged into the "MIDI-OUT" port of the master keyboard. The other end of the cable is then plugged into the "MIDI-IN" port of the slave. The MIDI controls on the master will be set to "MIDI TRANSMIT," while the MIDI controls on the slave will be set to "MIDI RECEIVE." A choice of one of sixteen channels is selected on the master keyboard for the transmission of MIDI musical data (notes played, pitch bend, foot pedal, etc.). The master keyboard will be the "sender." The MIDI keyboard which will be accepting the information sent to it from the master keyboard will be called the "receiver."

The MIDI "receiver" has two modes of operation. The first mode is called the "OMNI" mode, which allows the keyboard to receive MIDI information on any or all of the available sixteen channels—at the same time. This may not be desired, however, because in this mode the MIDI "receiver" may be playing and processing musical parts not intended for it to "listen to"—a condition present when a MIDI multi-track digital sequencer is used as the master, instead of a keyboard. (Digital sequencers are used in more advanced MIDI setups, and are covered in detail later in the text.) The "OMNI" mode is then switched to the "POLY" mode which allows only one of the sixteen available MIDI channels to be selected.

For example, if the MIDI keyboard which is sending musical information is set to transmit on MIDI channel three and is then played, the receiver keyboard which is hooked up to the sending keyboard via a MIDI cable must be set to receive on MIDI channel three in order for the second keyboard (receiver) to be played by the first keyboard (sender).

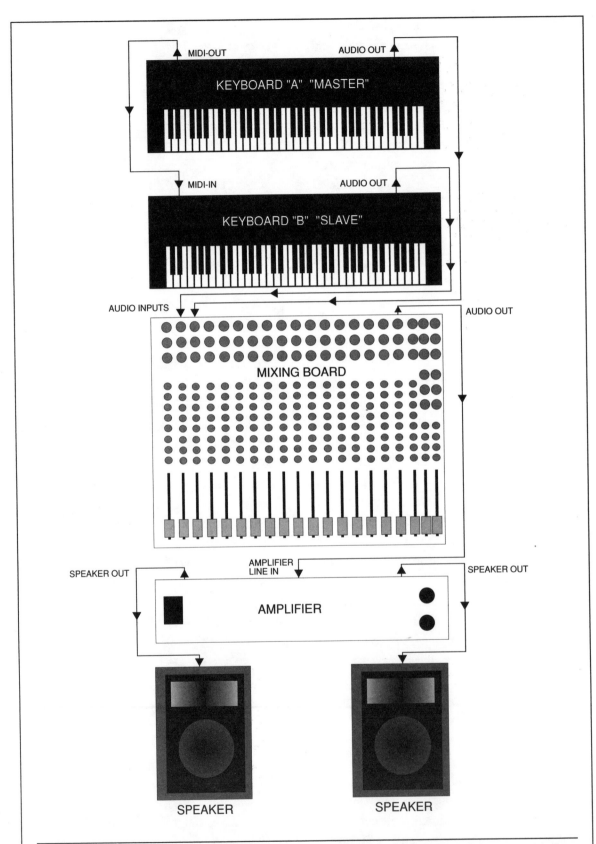

Figure 1. A basic MIDI setup. With a MIDI cable connected from the MIDI-OUT port of keyboard "A" to the MIDI-IN port of keyboard "B," keyboard "B" will sound together with keyboard "A" when keyboard "A" is played. This basic use of MIDI is called a "master/slave" configuration.

(master) keyboard automatically plays or "triggers" the same notes on the second (slave) keyboard. If the first electronic keyboard is set to play a string sound, and the second electronic keyboard is set for a brass sound, or "patch" as it is often called, the sounds of both instruments playing the same part will simultaneously be heard. Voilà — instant orchestration!

## The Electronic Orchestra

Now that we have a general idea of how electronic musical instruments can "interface" to make beautiful music through the use of MIDI, let's continue to build our electronic orchestra and add still more electronic instruments.

The most fascinating aspect of connecting MIDI instruments together is the use of the MIDI-THRU port. The MIDI-THRU port allows multiple electronic musical instruments to be connected together, one after the other, in a chain. This is known as a "daisy chain." A daisy chain is created by first selecting a master or "host" instrument, and plugging a five-pin DIN cable (which is often supplied with MIDI-equipped instruments by the manufacturer) into the port located on the rear panel of the instrument labeled MIDI-OUT. The other end of the cable is then connected to the MIDI-IN port of the first instrument to be used in the chain. To continue the daisy chain, it now becomes necessary to use a second MIDI cable. Simply connect one end of the cable into the MIDI-THRU port of the second electronic keyboard in the chain. Then, take the other end of the MIDI cable and plug it into the MIDI-IN port of the third electronic keyboard. In general, the MIDI-THRU port is used when there are more than two electronic instruments in the system. The digital information is sent from the master instrument using a MIDI cable connected to its MIDI-OUT port, to the second instrument using the other end of the MIDI cable connected to its MIDI-IN port. By using a second MIDI cable connected to the second electronic instrument's MIDI-THRU port, the digital data that is being sent from the master instrument is allowed to pass through the second instrument — unchanged and unaffected — to the third receiving electronic instrument. Now, anything played on the master instrument will be recognized, deciphered and performed on the second and third instruments as well. This third electronic instrument could also be an electronic keyboard, perhaps set to play a bell sound (if it is so equipped), and, when combined with the string sound from the first keyboard and the brass sound from the second keyboard, will produce an orchestral sound texture that is absolutely wonderful!

It is important to understand that the MIDI connections are completely independent of the audio (sound) connections. The MIDI ports allow for the transmission and reception of digital information *only*, and do not contain any portion of the sound output. Connections for audio (sound) output into some type of amplification system must still be made in order to hear any of the music being played (again, see figure 1).

To prevent any operating problems, make sure that the cables used for MIDI connection are MIDI spec. cables (that is, cables that are designed specifically for MIDI use), not the five-pin DIN cables found in some audio stores. Though these audio store five-pin DIN cables may work, they are not designed specifically for MIDI applications. It's not worth risking the frustration of hooking up all of your beautiful music-making gear, playing the instruments, and having no sound come out of the speakers. That would certainly put a damper on a potential spark of creativity!

If the MIDI-THRU box using three keyboards daisy chained together proves to be inadequate in terms of music power (although in most simple MIDI setups three can be just fine), and a fourth or even fifth sound source is needed, it becomes necessary to introduce a device into the MIDI system known as a MIDI-THRU box. Daisy chaining more than three MIDI devices together introduces a noticeable time delay between the time a key is played on the master keyboard and the time the sound from the fourth keyboard is heard, if the fourth keyboard's MIDI-IN port is connected to the third MIDI keyboard's MIDI-THRU port in the normal daisy chain manner. The time delay occurs because it takes a small amount of time to process the information coming into the MIDI-IN port before the information can be set out to the MIDI-THRU port. Even though, as mentioned earlier, the information sent to the MIDI-THRU port is unchanged and unaffected, the time delay still occurs. This small delay is actually present even when daisy chaining two keyboards together, but it really does not become noticeable until after three keyboards or other MIDI instruments are connected.

The MIDI-THRU box eliminates any noticeable time delays because it consists of a single MIDI-IN port and multiple MIDI-THRU ports—usually up to eight. The connection is really very simple. First, plug a MIDI cable into the MIDI-OUT port of the master keyboard. Then, connect the other end of the MIDI cable into the MIDI-IN port of the MIDI-THRU box. Each additional MIDI instrument is then connected to the MIDI-THRU ports provided on the rear panel of the MIDI-THRU box. The MIDI-THRU box sends as many as eight output signals simultaneously, thus eliminating any timing problems or noticeable delays in sound.

## MIDI Messages

MIDI is capable of transmitting and receiving a variety of unique "messages" along with the information which relates to key strokes, note duration, sustain pedal use, etc. These messages (which also are in the form of digital information) are special messages that relate to the internal functions and special features of electronic musical instruments—functions and features not found on traditional acoustic instruments.

Pitch bending is one such feature found on many of today's electronic keyboards. Pitch bend-

ing allows the user to literally bend the pitch of a note up and/or down a preset amount, the interval of which is determined by the player. The intervals are in half-step increments called semitones. The maximum range of pitch bending allowed for most electronic keyboards is plus or minus twelve semi-tones, which translates into plus or minus one full octave of pitch change. The pitch bending is controlled from the front of the electronic keyboard by using either a joystick or a pitch wheel of some kind, located to the left of the playing keys.

Another feature found on most of today's modern electronic keyboards is the ability to apply "modulation" to notes that are being played. The word "modulation" sounds rather technical—and it is. Simply stated, however, modulation creates movement in a sound. If the type of modulation used is pitch modulation, the end result will have movement in the pitch, or what is commonly known as "vibrato." Pitch modulation = vibrato. There are other forms of modulation as well. Modulation to make the sound move from a rich, brilliant timbre, towards a muffled "dark" sounding timbre is known as "filter modulation" (more about what a filter is a little later). Modulation that makes the sound move from a softer volume to a louder volume is called "amplitude modulation." Amplitude, in this case, refers to the amount of volume, or loudness, that is present.

There are still more kinds of information relating to the playing of notes that are recognized by MIDI. When an electronic MIDI keyboard is played, and the dynamics (softness and loudness) of the playing are recognized by MIDI, the keyboard is said to be "touch sensitive." Key or note "velocity" touch sensitivity is one such example of digital information that travels down the MIDI cable. Velocity (meaning "speed") touch sensitivity is what determines how loud or soft the notes being played will sound. Velocity touch sensitivity detects how quickly a key, when struck, travels from its resting "up" position, to its fully depressed "down" position. The harder a key is struck, the faster the key travels from its "up" position to its "down" position, and the louder the sound coming from the speakers will be. The inverse is true as well. The softer a key is stroked, the more time it takes for the key to travel from the "up" position to the "down" position, and the sound coming from the speakers will be softer. The dynamic response of velocity touch sensitivity mimics the dynamics of an acoustic piano.

Another form of touch sensitivity is "after-touch." After-touch is touch sensitivity that is sensed when a single key or chord is held down after being played, and then further pressure is applied to the key(s). When this pressure is applied, the sound will change in direct proportion to the amount of pressure applied. This is also known as "pressure" touch sensitivity. This pressure sensitivity can be directed to control amplitude (volume) — the harder the notes are leaned on, the louder the sound. It may also be set to control pitch — the harder the keys are pushed, the greater the change in pitch. The pitch change may be set to travel in either direction — up in pitch, or down in pitch. After-touch sensitivity can be programmed to control the filter (which governs how rich or muted the sound will be) as well. We will cover filters soon when we discuss how synthesizers generate sound.

Now that we have a basic working knowledge of MIDI and what it does, let's examine the many different types of MIDI instruments, what they do, and their application to MIDI music making.

## Synthesizers

Electronic keyboards are the most popular tools for composing and performing music through MIDI. Just about any sound, whether natural or synthetic, can be created or duplicated by these electronic keyboards. MIDI electronic keyboards are actually electronic "synthesizers," because that is really the way they generate sounds. The sounds are electronically synthesized (artificially created) and then played from the synthesizer's keyboard. There are several different ways to electronically synthesize sounds. One method of electronic musical sound synthesis is not intended to replace another, because each form of electronic sound synthesis has its own sonic (sound) "personality" (see figure 2). As figure 2 indicates, there are two basic categories of electronic musical synthesis: analog synthesis and digital synthesis.

### Analog synthesis

Analog synthesizers were the first synthesizers commercially available and mass-produced, entering the music scene back in the late 1960s. There were other electronic music synthesizers (which were also analog) in use back in the 1940s and 1950s, but these synthesizers were cumbersome and occupied the space of an average-sized living room! Needless to say, they were not very practical and had little appeal to the gigging or even studio musician. These early electronic music synthesizers were really not very musical, as they didn't provide any real means of melodic playing; sound was changed by twiddling knobs, because there was no keyboard attached to them. The commercially available analog synthesizers of the 1960s were large, too, but smaller, portable versions of these synthesizers were created, which sparked a new era in electronic music that changed the course of the music industry and the way we look at music today.

Analog synthesizers are voltage-controlled synthesizers. Their sounds are generated by oscillators and changed in direct proportion to varying voltages applied to those oscillators. The greater the voltage, the higher the pitch of the sound. The opposite is true as well; less voltage generates a sound which is lower in pitch.

Once the sound is generated, "shaping" of the sound is needed. At this point we have a "raw" sound with no character or identifiable qualities. The sound has no special "color."

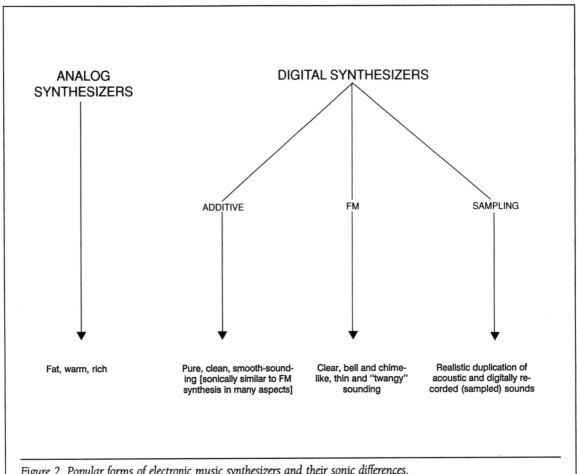

ANALOG SYNTHESIZERS

DIGITAL SYNTHESIZERS

ADDITIVE

FM

SAMPLING

Fat, warm, rich

Pure, clean, smooth-sounding [sonically similar to FM synthesis in many aspects]

Clear, bell and chime-like, thin and "twangy" sounding

Realistic duplication of acoustic and digitally re-corded (sampled) sounds

*Figure 2. Popular forms of electronic music synthesizers and their sonic differences.*

Shaping of the sound is achieved by manipulating two elements.

The first of these two shaping elements is the filter. The filter dictates whether the sound will be crystal clear, or whether it will be muffled and muted. The filter is actually similar to the "treble" and "bass" tone controls found on your home stereo system. If the music is either too crisp or not crisp enough, the "treble" control allows you to adjust the high-frequency (high pitch) content of the music, to suit your specific needs. Similarly, if the overall sound of the music is too "boomy" sounding, or if more low frequencies (low pitch) are needed to reinforce the sound, the "bass" control is used to doctor up the tone. The type of filter found on most of today's electronic synthesizers is called a "low-pass" filter. The low-

pass filter does what its name implies. It allows low frequencies (low tones) to pass through it, while blocking the passage of high frequencies (high tones). The point at which the high frequencies will be blocked out can be set by the user. This point is called the "cut-off" point. This high-frequency blocking is what determines the richness of a sound. For example, a synthesized electronic string sound will allow more high-frequency sound to pass through the filter. The end result is a sound that is rich in "harmonics." [Harmonics (also known as "overtones") are a series of upper-frequency (higher pitched) tones that give a particular sound its richness and crispness. A cymbal crash is another good example of a sound that is rich in harmonics.] Synthesized sounds, like muted horns, oboes, xylophones and flutes, are all examples of sounds that use a lower setting for the filter cut-off. This in turn restricts the amount of harmonics (remember — upper-frequency overtones) that are permitted to pass through the low-pass filter, creating a duller, less crisp, even solemn sound.

The second element responsible for shaping a sound is the envelope generator. This is the section of a synthesizer that instructs a sound when to begin being heard (after a key is depressed), and when to end. The word "envelope" is used to describe the "curve" that represents the journey a sound takes as it travels between these beginning and ending points. All sorts of fascinating things (with respect to volume level and sound color) could take place at any point in time between the beginning of the sound and the end of the sound. The word "generator" simply means to generate, or to produce. The envelope generator may be set so that there is a delay between the pressing of a key and the sounding of its note, or it may be set so that the note will be heard immediately.

The control on the envelope generator section of the synthesizer which sets the amount of time it takes for a sound to be heard (after a key is depressed) is called the "attack" control. The "attack" control deals with just the beginning of a sound and is a function of time. The next portion of a sound's envelope is called its "decay." When a note on the keyboard is played and held down, the "attack" portion of the sound is heard first. Next, the sound can be tailored to slowly or quickly "drop off" in volume. This "dropping off" of volume while a note is being held down is called the "decay" time. An acoustic piano is a good example of an instrument with a slow decay time, which occurs naturally when notes are played and held down. As indicated, a sound's decay is also a function of time. A note held down on a piano normally drops down in volume to a point of inaudibility — that is the characteristic decay of an acoustic piano.

If so desired, the decay of a synthesizer's sound can be set to fall to a certain level of volume, and then remain at that volume until the note(s) being held down is released. This level of volume is called the "sustain" level and can be set as high or as low as needed. The "sustain" level differs from the "attack" time and the "decay" time in the sense that it is a function that relates to the amount of volume, not time. After a sound travels through the envelope stages and settles in to the "sustain" level, the note(s) being held down must be released. This brings us to the fourth and final stage of the envelope generator — the "release" stage. The "release" setting dictates the amount of time it takes for the remaining sound to fall to a level of "0" when the note(s) being played is released, or in other words, it determines the amount of time necessary for the sound to end (see figure 3).

The envelope generator is not limited to just controlling how loud a sound will be and how long the sound lasts.

The controlling functions of time and level of the envelope generator may be applied to the filter and to pitch as well, in addition to the loudness. If used to control the filter, the overall clarity and brilliance of a sound can be shaped with the envelope generator. When a note is played, for

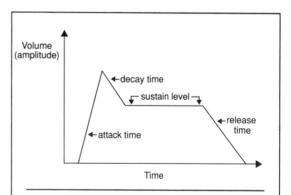

Figure 3. Behavior of the envelope generator. The attack time raises the signal to a specific level when a key is pressed. The decay time drops the level of the signal to a given holding level — the sustain level — while a key is held down. When the key is released, the level of the signal drops, at a given rate, to 0. All time and level values mentioned are fully adjustable.

example, the envelope generator may be set so that the sound begins as a muted or muffled sound, then gets crisper and crisper until it is very rich with harmonics. The envelope generator could have its "release" control set so that after the note is released, as the sound trails off, it becomes more and more muffled, until the sound eventually ends. Pitch can be controlled in the same manner. The envelope generator can be set so that the pitch of the sound rises up to, or falls down to, a set pitch when the keys are struck. That pitch could be left to remain constant while holding the keys down and then rise up, fall down, or even remain the same when the keys are released. The possibilities and combinations are endless!

Analog synthesizers have a very distinctive sonic (meaning sound) "color." Because of the presence of many harmonics, analog synthesizers are well suited for rich string-like synthesized sounds, as well as for rich brass sound textures. However, another quality that analog synthesizers possess is the ability to generate new and exciting sound colors—sounds that do not even remotely resemble the instruments of a traditional orchestra, or *any* sound that occurs in nature, for that matter! This is the real strength of analog synthesizers. Though they have the ability to generate electronic string sounds that are rich-sounding and even beautiful, the strings don't quite sound completely realistic. They sound nice, but not realistic. However, that is not a problem when using MIDI; in fact, it actually becomes an advantage—an advantage we will illustrate shortly.

Analog synthesizers in general are best known for their "fatness" and "warmth" of sound. This is because of the way sound synthesis is achieved. Analog synthesis uses a process known as "subtractive" or "filtering" synthesis. The raw elements of the sound are rich and full of harmonics. To design the various sounds, a filter combined with one or more envelope generators (sound familiar?) is used. This combination removes some of the excessive higher harmonics

(these higher harmonics tend to be a little "buzzy" sounding anyway), as well as shaping the sound into something that is musically useful. The type of filter most widely used in analog synthesis is the "low-pass" filter which, if you recall, allows all of the lower (bass) frequencies to pass through it, while selectively blocking out the higher frequencies. This is the main reason why analog synthesizers are known for their "fatness" and "warmth"—because the lower frequencies are permitted to continually pass through the filter into the amplification system or tape deck.

## Digital synthesis

Digital synthesizers were first introduced to the electronic music industry in the early 1980s, not long, actually, before the introduction of MIDI. Digital synthesizers opened up a whole new world of sonic possibilities. Because of the endless possibilities of digital synthesis, all kinds of new sound textures could be realized. There are many different forms of digital synthesis, and each is unique.

The original method of digital synthesis is called "additive" synthesis. Additive synthesis creates sounds by combining many pure electronic tones known as "sine-wave oscillators." A sine wave (in musical synthesis) is a pure musical sound. A sine wave is very smooth-sounding because it has no "buzzy" harmonics present. An oscillator is simply the part of any synthesizer—either analog or digital, that actually generates the sound itself. It makes the original "raw" sound. The idea of additive synthesis is this: If enough of these pure tones are added together—each tuned to a specific frequency (pitch) which represents harmonics, any sound can be "put together" by building it from the ground level up. Unfortunately, this is not a very practical means of digital synthesis because it would require many of these pure tones—hundreds of them, each with its own envelope generator, to effectively reproduce any natural sound. However, if an unnatural sound (that is, a sound that doesn't resemble anything acoustic that our ears are accustomed to hearing) is all that is needed, additive synthesis, in a limited sense, can yield some pretty interesting results.

A much more popular and widely used form of digital synthesis is called "frequency modulation" or FM synthesis. FM synthesis creates sounds by using oscillators or combinations of oscillators to control and electrically interact by digital means with other oscillators or combinations of oscillators. This interacting causes the oscillators to "color" each other, and different combinations yield different results in terms of sounds that will be heard. FM synthesizers are best known for their clarity of sound. Sounds like bells, chimes, marimbas, electric pianos and even "twangy" basses are characteristic of the variety of sounds that FM synthesis offers.

### Sampling synthesizers

Another popular form of digital synthesis is called "sampling." Sampling is the process by which a sound is digitally recorded—not onto tape, but into the digital memory of an instrument (usually a keyboard). A microphone, which is plugged into an electrical receptacle known as a "jack," located on the rear panel of the instrument, is used to capture the desired sound—violin, horn, dog barking, etc. This sound can be altered, processed, or "tweaked," and then played from the instrument (for our example we'll use a keyboard). I know that probably sounds confusing, so let's backtrack a bit, and see step-by-step what all of this means, and how the idea of sound processing or "tweaking" is musically useful.

First, it's important to point out the difference between other forms of digital synthesis and sampling. Additive synthesis and FM synthesis do exactly what their names imply—they synthesize or artificially create sounds. Sampling, on the other hand, uses sounds that already exist in natural form—violins, horns, dogs barking, etc., and allows them to be electronically "placed" into an electronic musical instrument, and then musi-cally performed and played from that instrument. A digital sampling keyboard is really a computer with black and white keys. I say this because when a microphone is plugged in and used to record a sound, the recorded sound is stored in the keyboard's computer memory. It's almost like taking a digital "snapshot" of a sound. Once there, the sound is treated as digital information, and can be manipulated the same way a regular computer accesses and changes files. The pitch of the sound can be altered, and even the "envelope" (remember envelopes?) can be changed. A sampled piano, for example, could have its "attack" time set so that when played from the keyboard, the sound has a slower entry time and not a hard percussive quality which is characteristic of the original acoustic piano sample. This creates a "bowing" effect, and makes the piano sample sound as if it were being played using a violin bow, instead of from the black and white keys. Voilà, a bowed piano!

An interesting feature of sampling is that a single note of a sound can be sampled—we'll use the acoustic piano for our example—and then played from the sampling keyboard in a chordal fashion, that is, chords consisting of more than just the original note can be played at the same time from the sampling keyboard. This is known as "polyphonic" playing. "Poly" means "many," and "phonic" means "sound." Polyphonic = many sounds.

The micro-processor (computer) in the sampling keyboard allows the digital data which represents the sampled sound to be "read-back" from computer memory at different rates, depending on which notes on the keyboard are being played. It is very much like playing a 33⅓ RPM phonograph record (remember those?). If a note played on the keyboard is higher than the original sampled pitch, it will be read from the keyboard's computer memory at a faster rate, which is very similar to playing the same record at 78 RPM. If a note is played on the keyboard that is lower than the original sampled pitch, the data will be read from the sampling keyboard's computer memory at a much slower rate of speed, and the result is a lower pitch which is equivalent to playing the phonograph record at 16 RPM. If a human voice is used as the source for sampling, and a note on the sampling keyboard is played that corresponds to the original pitch of the human voice sample, the sound heard would be identical to that which was sampled. However, if a note on the sampling keyboard is played that is much higher than the original note of the human voice sample, the sound heard would be something that resembles Donald Duck! If a note on the sampling keyboard is played that is much lower than the original note of the human voice sample, the end result would sound something like a hippopotamus yawning in slow motion!

The main difference between sampling keyboards and other types of digital and even analog synthesizers is one of realism in sound. Because a sampling keyboard's sounds originate from natural sources (i.e. violin, saxophone, guitar, horn, human voice), the resulting sound is very realistic.

Most of today's electronic MIDI keyboards are actually "hybrids," consisting of elements found on both digital and analog synthesizers. Most digital keyboards use envelope generators and filters, found on the traditional analog synthesizers. This allows them to use whatever form of digital sound generation the manufacturer may choose, while having the added benefit and flexibility of analog processing—processing which is considered to be relatively user-friendly.

## Drum Machines

The next most popular electronic musical instrument used in MIDI is the digital drum machine. The digital drum machine usually has forty-nine or more "sampled" drum and percussion sounds stored it its internal digital memory. These sounds can be programmed, by tapping on buttons located on the front panel of the instrument which correspond to the various drum sounds, to play in

various rhythmic patterns—usually up to ninety-nine patterns. The patterns can then be chained together to form completed songs. The digital drum machine has an electronic metronome built into it that serves as a master timekeeper, also known as its "clock." This "clock" provides a timing reference when programming the various drum patterns. The digital drum machine can also accept a "clock" from an external MIDI device, such as a digital MIDI sequencer (which we will cover shortly), allowing its tempo (speed) to be controlled by the external MIDI device.

Digital drum machines have incorporated into their design the ability to automatically, instantaneously fix any timing mistakes made during the programming of drum patterns. This automatic timing adjusting is called "error-correction," also known as "quantization." The quantization value, or amount of error-correction that is used, can be set for a particular note value. For example, if the error-correction is set at sixteenth notes, any timing mistakes made during drum pattern programming would be automatically shifted or "pulled" to the nearest sixteenth note when listening back to the part.

Digital drum machines also allow their internal pre-sampled drum sounds to be played or "triggered" from an external MIDI keyboard. Certain keys on the MIDI keyboard are assigned to trigger the different drum sounds in the drum machine via MIDI. The drum machine sounds are also assigned to correspond to those keys on the MIDI keyboard.

Usual drum "note" assignments set the bass drum sound in the digital drum machine to respond to the note "C1" (which is the lowest "C" note) on the MIDI keyboard; "D1" is used for the snare drum sound; "F#1" for the closed high-hat sound; "A#1" for the open high-hat sound; "C#1" for the sidestick; and "D#1" is used for the handclaps. The "crash" cymbal is often assigned to "C#2," while the "ride" cymbal is often assigned to "D#1." The drum machine tom-toms are generally assigned to "F1," "A1" and

"C2." All of these digital drum machine note assignments are typical. However, any notes may be used, as long as the digital drum machine and the MIDI keyboard are both set to the same note numbers for any given sound. All other drum sounds and percussion sounds can be selectively assigned as well. Once assigned, the digital drum machine can then receive information sent on one of the sixteen MIDI channels from the MIDI keyboard. It's important to remember that in order for the two MIDI instruments to properly "communicate" with each other, they must both be assigned to the same MIDI channel.

## More MIDI Instruments

There are a few "specialty" MIDI instruments. The first is the MIDI guitar controller. The MIDI guitar controller is similar to an electric guitar, in that it looks something like an electric guitar and has six strings that are played like those on an electric guitar. However, the MIDI guitar controller has a "MIDI-OUT" port, which allows the musical notes played on the guitar strings to be converted into digital information that is recognized by MIDI. The MIDI guitar controller is used in much the same way as the MIDI keyboard. The main (and obvious) difference is that the MIDI guitar controller uses guitar strings to transmit MIDI information, while the MIDI keyboard uses the black and white keys to transmit MIDI information to the other MIDI devices in the chain.

The next and most widely used MIDI "specialty" device is the MIDI "expander." A MIDI "expander" is essentially a MIDI keyboard without the keys. It contains all of the same internal electronics as MIDI synthesizers, but without the physical keys. There is really no need for the keys. This is because when daisy-chaining multiple MIDI synthesizers together, the only synthesizer required to have the physical black and white keys is the first synthesizer in the chain. The first synthesizer is the only synthesizer that is played. It serves as the transmitter of MIDI information. The other synthesizers in the chain are all receiv-

ers of the MIDI information sent out from the transmitter. The only MIDI ports used for the expanders, then, would be the MIDI-IN ports, and the MIDI-THRU ports. An obvious advantage of using expanders instead of synthesizers (with the full-range physical keyboard) is the small amount of space they occupy. Because a MIDI expander is essentially the "brain" of a synthesizer only, a much smaller case or cabinet is required to house the internal electronics. Most MIDI expanders are a standard rack-mount width of only nineteen inches. Because most electronic musical instrument manufacturers adhere to building their MIDI expanders to this standard rack-mount width, many different expanders from various electronic musical instrument manufacturers can be mounted in the same rack, which is a real convenience to most musicians. The number of MIDI expanders housed in the rack simply depends on the size of your pocketbook! MIDI expanders are still relatively cheap compared to full-sized synthesizers (see figure 4).

| Product | Price Range |
|---|---|
| Electronic Keyboards— Including all types of sound synthesis and sampling | $800-3,000 |
| MIDI Expanders— Including all types of sound synthesis and sampling | $200-2,000 |
| Digital Drum Machines | $250-1,000 |
| MIDI Guitars | $200-1,500 |
| MIDI Signal Processors— Including digital delay, digital reverb, and digital multi-effects processors | $400-2,000 |
| MIDI Wind Controllers | $100-500 |
| MIDI Thru Box | $60-100 |

Figure 4. Typical prices of average electronic MIDI instruments (1991).

MIDI expanders are especially suited for guitar controllers, because, since the guitar strings function as the means of transmitting MIDI information, full-sized synthesizers (with their playing keys) are never needed. MIDI guitar controllers allow each string to individually transmit performance information on a different MIDI channel. Many MIDI synthesizer expanders (and full-sized keyboards, for that matter) have a special feature which allows them to receive MIDI information on more than one MIDI channel at the same time. This is ideal for the reception of MIDI information sent from guitar controllers, and keyboard synthesizers as well. When a synthesizer or expander uses this multi-channel function, it is said to be receiving MIDI information in the "multi-timbral" mode of operation. This simply means that the MIDI synthesizer or expander is capable of receiving many channels of MIDI performance information (different musical parts). It is then able to generate more than one of its internal sounds (strings, brass and a bass sound for example) at the same time. Each sound is set on a different MIDI channel, in order to accommodate the various musical parts being sent through MIDI from the master MIDI transmitter. This function is best utilized when using a MIDI digital "sequencer," which we will be discussing shortly.

There are still other "specialty" MIDI devices worth mentioning. One is the MIDI "breath-controller" (also known as a "wind-controller") which plugs into a special hole found on some synthesizers and allows the synthesized sound to be articulated by blowing through a plastic tube (perfect for horn and wind instrument players) while holding down notes on the keyboard. Another "specialty" device is the "MIDI master keyboard" which has no internal sounds of its own, but is used strictly as a master transmitter of MIDI information. The master keyboard provides advanced MIDI functions such as multiple keyboard "splits"—the ability to create different playing "zones," each capable of transmitting performance information on a separate MIDI channel—and individual zone pitch transposing, which allows the pitch of a particular playing zone to be changed without affecting the pitch of the other playing zones. Because the "MIDI master controller" has no internal sounds of its own, and is always used as a transmitter of MIDI information only, it is always placed first in the MIDI daisy chain.

## The MIDI Sequencer

The nucleus of any MIDI setup is a digital event recording device known as the digital "sequencer." The digital sequencer is to MIDI what a multi-track tape recorder is to acoustic sounds. Digital sequencers have the ability to record any and all types of MIDI information. It's important to understand the differences between MIDI event recording, which is what a digital sequencer does, and multi-track tape recording. Digital sequencers record MIDI information ONLY, and cannot record the sounds picked up by a microphone, or sounds from other "line" sources such as a compact disc player or phonograph. With sampling, however, it is possible to use a microphone to record a sound which is then converted into MIDI information. This MIDI information, when played from a MIDI keyboard, for example, could then be recorded into the MIDI sequencer, because the MIDI information is now in the form of a "language" that the MIDI sequencer understands, and when played back, the sequencer will drive the MIDI instrument, playing the sampled sound. Many different tracks of MIDI recording are possible with the digital sequencer, just as many tracks of recording are possible with a multi-track tape recorder—but the similarities of the two recording mediums pretty much end there.

Before the introduction of MIDI, musicians relied on the use of two-, four-, and eight-track tape recorders as a means of assembling their musical compositions. Musical parts, and the sounds chosen for the musical parts had to be carefully considered before recording them onto tape. This is because many times a process known as "bouncing" became necessary, especially when recording was done on the smaller format two-track and four-track tape recorders.

"Bouncing" occurs when two or more tracks of recorded music are combined and blended together, and then copied onto another "empty" track. For example, tracks one and two of a four-track multi-track tape recorder could be combined together and blended, and then copied onto track four. Track four now contains a mix of the recorded music that was on tracks one and two. This now frees up tracks one and two, which allows additional musical parts to be recorded onto them. The problem with bouncing is that once the tracks are combined and bounced together, they are locked into that particular blend of the original tracks. The bounce cannot be undone. Once the original tracks of music are erased and re-recorded over, there is nothing that can change the relationship of the blended tracks, should you decide that you are unhappy with the blend. This is a limitation of multi-track tape recording. Another drawback to bouncing when recording on tape is that the more you bounce, the more combined tape noise and "hiss" become evident, and the sound quality of the bounces deteriorates.

The MIDI sequencer, unlike a multi-track tape recorder, does not suffer from the problems of noise, tape "hiss," and deteriorating sound quality when bouncing tracks of MIDI performance information because you are bouncing MIDI data ONLY, not the actual sounds themselves.

## Sequencer operation

The principle of MIDI sequencer operation is simple. First, a musical part or melodic line is played on a MIDI keyboard, which has its MIDI-OUT port connected to the MIDI-IN port of the digital sequencer. All the keyboardist need do is assign any one of the sixteen MIDI channels available to the track that is being engaged for recording, push the "start" button to begin recording, and play the keyboard. The digital sequencer records the musical part played, and remembers it by storing it in its computer-based memory. When the sequencer's "play" button is pushed, the MIDI-OUT port of the sequencer sends out the recorded musical data to multiple MIDI expanders that are daisy chained together. (Don't forget that if more than three MIDI keyboards or expanders are used in the daisy chain, a MIDI-THRU box becomes necessary to eliminate audible timing delays.)

Many different tracks of musical data can be recorded into the MIDI sequencer, simply by choosing a track to be recorded on, selecting a MIDI channel that will be assigned to "listen to" and remember the musical information recorded on that track, and then repeating the process for as many tracks as are available, assigning each new recorded part to its appropriate MIDI channel. The effect of recording and playing back multiple MIDI tracks is similar to the effect of recording multiple tracks on a multi-track tape recorder. There is a major difference, however. When the "play" button of the MIDI sequencer is pushed, the MIDI keyboards, expanders and drum machine are essentially being played "live," because the digital information that represents the actual playing of the parts is being sent back to the individual MIDI keyboards, expanders and drum machine. The sound heard is not coming from tape, but from the "audio outputs" of the MIDI drum machine, keyboards and expanders themselves. It's as if they were being played for the first time. If any one of us had eight or even ten arms to play, it would create the same effect. This means that the volume of each instrument is always able to be adjusted because the sound of the music being played from the MIDI sequencer is coming from the individual MIDI instrument audio outputs, not from tape. The MIDI sequencer is very much like a digital "player piano."

The number of sequencer tracks on a digital

sequencer depends on the individual brand of sequencer. The number generally ranges from eight to sixty-four. However, there are some very high-end digital sequencers that have more than sixty-four tracks of MIDI event recording available.

### Channels vs. tracks

At this point, it's important to make sure that you have a clear understanding of the difference between MIDI channels and sequencer tracks. As mentioned earlier, there are sixteen MIDI channels available for the independent exchange of musical performance information, which is in the form of digital data. Remember, all sixteen channels of MIDI data can travel through a single MIDI cable, because if you recall, digital MIDI data travels in a serial fashion—one piece of musical data after another at an incredible rate of speed. This is how all sixteen channels of MIDI information can be "squeezed" through a single cable. The number of sequencer tracks available, as previously mentioned, can be greater than sixty-four.

This is where it gets a little tricky. Let's use a musical example to illustrate the difference between sequencer tracks and MIDI channels. Let's assume we've already recorded some basic music tracks. The drums, bass part and a piano part have already been recorded into the MIDI sequencer. [Don't forget that a digital drum machine can be used as a MIDI expander because its internal drum sounds can be played externally from a MIDI keyboard. The other option for recording drum parts is to do all of the drum programming within the drum machine by creating drum patterns and then chaining them together. The next step would be to synchronize the drum machine with the MIDI sequencer by setting the drum machine's "clock" to accept the clock rate put out by the MIDI sequencer (the MIDI sequencer also has a built-in electronic metronome that serves as its timekeeper). The MIDI-OUT port of the sequencer, though it may go through a daisy chain or MIDI-THRU box, eventually finds its way to the MIDI-IN port of the drum machine.]

With the drums, bass and piano already recorded, it's time to overdub a new part—a string line, let's say. First we'll select a sequencer track to record on—any track will do. For our example we'll use track ten. It really makes no difference which track is selected; it's really a matter of how each musician chooses to work. Now we'll select MIDI channel three for the strings. Again, it makes absolutely no difference which MIDI channel is chosen for the new part; it's really a matter of personal preference and production approach. MIDI sequencers also have "quantization" for auto-correction of timing problems when playing (see the section on digital drum machines), but for our example we won't use any quantization, just to keep things simple. With track number and MIDI channel assigned, let's push the "record" button and begin playing.

Imagine that we made it halfway through the song when—oops, a wrong note was played. Let's assume the performance was nothing short of brilliant right up until the point at which the mistake was made. Naturally, we will want to save the good stuff and eliminate the mistake. This is where the power of sequencer editing, which we will cover next, comes into play. Once the mistake is eliminated, we now have an acceptable string track with the exception of the fact that it is incomplete (remember, we stopped halfway through). If we then take track eleven and assign it to MIDI channel three, which is the same MIDI channel that track ten (which contains the string part for the first half of the song) is on, we can continue playing the string part for the second half of the song. Since both sequencer tracks ten and eleven are assigned to the same MIDI channel, the MIDI keyboard or expander assigned to "listen" to information on MIDI channel three will play the two string tracks as one continuous string part, because both tracks are sending out MIDI data from the sequencer on MIDI channel three. That's the basic difference between sequencer tracks and MIDI channels. Any number of tracks may be assigned to the same MIDI channel.

This is especially useful when programming drum tracks into the sequencer. The bass drum could be recorded on track twelve, for example, the snare drum on track thirteen, the high-hat on track fourteen, and the tom-toms on track fifteen. If all of the drum tracks are assigned to MIDI channel sixteen, and the drum machine is also set to receive information on MIDI channel sixteen, the drum machine will recognize and play all of the drum parts on sequencer tracks twelve, thirteen, fourteen and fifteen. If more sequencer tracks are needed for additional musical parts, the drum tracks, since they are all assigned to the same MIDI channel, could be bounced together. This process of bouncing is called track "merging." You see, practically speaking, only one instrument part is recorded at a time on any given sequencer track. If you try to record another part on that track, the original performance information will be erased. This is why the drum parts are often recorded on separate tracks. A full drum kit can be played by overdubbing on many different sequencer tracks. After the full drum part is recorded on the different sequencer tracks, the tracks may be "merged" together without affecting any aspect of the individual drum parts. The "merged" track which is assigned to MIDI channel sixteen (for our example) now contains the MIDI data for ALL of the drum parts. Now you can begin to see why many tracks may be needed for MIDI recording.

### Sequencer editing

When assembling a song, it sometimes becomes necessary to alter some of the musical parts after they have been recorded into the digital sequencer. Whether it is "repairing" wrong notes, changing the "register" (pitch) of a track, adding or removing measures of the song (which affects the song's length), a variety of "editing" options found in most digital sequencers can be used to alter any existing MIDI data. The "delete" func-

tion allows you to selectively remove any wrong notes played by deleting (erasing) them from a track. The "delete" function may also be used to remove any number of measures of the song, which shortens the length of the song. The "insert" function is used to add more measures to the song which, of course, lengthens the song. The "insert" function may also be used to insert additional notes into a sequencer track. The process by which individual notes are inserted into a sequencer track is known as "step-time" programming. Step-time programming allows you to put together a musical part by entering one note at a time into a track on the sequencer. When finished, this track may be played together with any other tracks that were recorded in "real-time." Real-time recording is the normal method of recording a track. It simply means that the musical parts played into the sequencer were performed in real, or normal time.

Another unique feature that digital sequencers possess is the ability to create "time compression," and "time expansion." Time compression means that the tempo (speed) of a recorded sequence (song) may be speeded up, making the song shorter, without affecting the pitch of the music. Time expansion means that the tempo of a recorded sequence may be slowed down, making the song longer, also without affecting the pitch of the music.

### Advanced MIDI features

Many other advanced editing features are offered on the more expensive sequencers. One such feature is the ability to take any piece of recorded MIDI data and change it into some other type of MIDI data. For example, all "C#1" notes can be changed to "D#1" notes by using an editing function called the "transform" function. If the "C#1" notes and the "D#1" notes recorded are on a drum track, that means that the "sidestick" notes ("C#1") would now be "handclaps" ("D#1").

Another advanced function of MIDI sequencers is "MIDI automation." MIDI automation allows certain changes in MIDI data to be recorded onto a track, so that when playing the recorded sequence back, these changes happen automatically. MIDI volume level mixing is the best example of MIDI automation. The volume level of MIDI keyboards, expanders and the drum machine may be controlled via MIDI. Any changes in volume may be recorded as special data onto a track in the sequencer which is designated as the "control" track (as opposed to a track that contains musical data). The actual instrument "mix" of a song can be fully automated, which means that when the audio output of the mixing board is "patched" into a stereo two-track tape recorder or a digital DAT machine, all you have to do is push the "record" button on the mix-down machine and the "play" button on the sequencer, and sit back and let the music mix itself!

Functions such as "program change" can be automated as well. As mentioned earlier, most synthesizers (which includes expanders) are shipped from the factory with many sounds stored in their internal memory. These sounds will usually range from strings to flutes to cosmic sound effects. These sounds are referred to as "programs." Programs on a synthesizer, expander, drum machine or MIDI digital effects unit (a MIDI digital effects unit contains sound processing programs such as digital delay and digital reverb), can be changed from one to another by means of an external source, such as another synthesizer or digital sequencer, via MIDI. When the sequencer is used, these program changes may be recorded as MIDI "control" information (instead of musical information) into one of the available tracks of the sequencer. When the sequencer "play" button is pushed, the program changes that were recorded for a given synthesizer, expander, drum machine or MIDI digital effects unit will occur automatically. MIDI control information is treated the same way that MIDI musical information is treated. In order for MIDI volume

control or MIDI program changes to happen, the instrument(s) that are being affected must be assigned to the same MIDI channel as the "control" track of the MIDI sequencer that contains the volume control or program change information.

**Sequencer hardware and software**
MIDI sequencers, as mentioned earlier, are computer-based devices and come in two different forms. The first type of MIDI sequencer is the "hardware" sequencer. This is a dedicated unit that is built and housed in its own case. "Hardware" means that it is a physical piece of gear. The second type of MIDI sequencer is the "software" sequencer. Software is the information that represents a particular computer program and is stored on a floppy disk and loaded into a computer. Both sequencers perform essentially the same duties, and there are advantages and disadvantages to both hardware and software sequencers.

The advantage of using a hardware sequencer is its portability. Because it is a dedicated unit built into its own housing, the hardware sequencer may be easily transported for "live" use on the stage. Yes, sequencers are often used on stage these days to provide music backup for performing acts. The disadvantage of hardware sequencers is that they have fewer of the advanced features found on computer software sequencers and a lot less memory.

The advantage of a computer software sequencing program over a hardware sequencer is that the computer has far greater memory capacity than the hardware sequencer. This means that much more information can reside in the computer's internal memory than in the hardware sequencer's memory. Even though the "brain" of the hardware sequencer is actually a microcomputer, its memory capacity does not match that of a regular computer. Software sequencing programs also have many more options and editing features than hardware sequencers.

An obvious disadvantage of the software sequencing program is that a computer is always needed to run the program. This makes transporting the entire system awkward and impractical. The second disadvantage of using a computer software sequencing program is having to pay the higher combined cost of both the computer and the sequencing program which is stored separately on a floppy disk.

There are other computer software programs written for MIDI in addition to software sequencing programs. This really makes the computer a worthwhile investment when putting together a medium to high-end MIDI studio. The most popular and widely used software program in addition to the software sequencing program for computers is the "patch librarian" program (patch = sound). The patch librarian program is a computer program that stores sounds and/or banks of sounds (via MIDI) from the various electronic musical instrument manufacturers, digital keyboards and expanders. The sounds to be saved to computer disk are transmitted through MIDI from the keyboards and expanders (some MIDI expanders have a MIDI-OUT port for this purpose) to the computer, using the computer's MIDI-IN port. This creates organized computer files providing fast accessibility to the sounds (because of the high speed of computers) and allows for massive computer disk storage of the sounds.

All MIDI sequencers, whether hardware or computer software, use floppy disks as a means to permanently store the recorded MIDI sequences. Sampling keyboards also use floppy disks to back up the contents of their internal memory. This is necessary because most sequencers—both hardware and computer—and sampling keyboards, lose the contents of their internal memory when the power is turned off. Once the necessary information is given its own file name and saved to disk, it can be recalled at any time by simply placing the disk into the disk drive of the sequencer or sampler (whichever is being used), and then loading in the appropriate file name. Another reason for saving recorded sequences and sampled sounds to floppy disk is to clear the internal mem-

ory of these devices so that more memory is available for new information.

## The Synchronizer

To complete any MIDI setup, a "synchronizer," which synchronizes the MIDI sequencer (whether hardware or software) to a standard multi-track tape recorder, is needed. This provides great flexibility when constructing a song, because the majority of the music may be recorded into the MIDI sequencer, and any acoustic instruments, electronic instruments not using MIDI, and vocals will be recorded on the multi-track tape recorder. A special synchronization "code" tone which contains information consisting of song start time, song tempo (in this case also known as "clock rate"), and song position (the location, with regard to time, of the song) is first recorded onto an empty track of the multi-track tape recorder. The synchronizer is then hooked up to both the MIDI sequencer and the multi-track tape recorder. When the tape recorder "play" button is pushed, the synchronizer "reads" the synchronization code which has been recorded onto a track of the multi-track tape recorder and sends this timing information to the MIDI sequencer, which is set to "read" external synchronization (usually abbreviated to "sync"). The two units "run" in perfect synchronization with each other. The audio outputs of the multi-track tape recorder, as well as the audio outputs for each of the MIDI keyboards, expanders and digital drum machine are all plugged into a mixing board. A two-track stereo tape recorder or digital DAT machine may now be used as the master mixdown machine, accepting a stereo "feed" from the output of the mixing board.

With MIDI, an entire electronic orchestra can be born—literally from within the boundaries of the home studio. From the "fat" timbre of analog-synthesized strings and brass, to the crisp cutting edge of FM bells and chimes—and let's not forget the realism of sampled timpani and drums—the potential of MIDI can be unleashed with full force, fulfilling the dreams and passions of songwriters from all walks. It is certainly encouraging to see so many manufacturers of electronic musical instruments working together in further developing the specifications of MIDI. No one is really sure what the future holds for MIDI, but songwriters and producers alike will certainly continue to create electronically orchestrated music, with the security of knowing that MIDI is here to stay.

•  •  •

## James Becher

James Becher is a seasoned multi-keyboardist/producer/composer who has worked with such artists as Jon Anderson (Yes), Verdine White (Earth, Wind and Fire), Ed Gagliardi (Foreigner) and Bobby Rondinelli (Rainbow). He served as product specialist and keyboard clinician with M.T.I. (Music Technology Inc.), working on the original "Synergy" project with Tom Piggott, Stoney Stockell and Wendy Carlos. He has also been a consultant to European keyboard manufacturers Crumar and Siel, and was involved with development and sound design of Korg's "M1-MIDI Workstation" electronic keyboard. *The Songwriter's and Musician's Guide to Making Great Demos*, published by Writer's Digest Books, lists James Becher as technical editor and consultant, and he has written for and been featured in *db Magazine*'s "Electronic Cottage." Becher currently owns and operates his music production company "Ariel Music Design" in East Northport, New York.

# The Art of Pitching Songs

TERI MUENCH

Whether you are a writer, manager of a songwriter, song plugger or publisher, learning how to pitch songs effectively will be crucial to your success. The exciting part of all this is that there are no set rules and there are so many avenues to explore. This allows you to be very creative in your approach. Through experience, you'll learn what works for you and what doesn't. I hope in sharing what I have learned that you will gain some insight and encouragement and find a clearer path to reach your goal.

## Making Contact

As your contacts grow in the industry, so will your chances of getting that special song you believe in noticed by the right artist. Working at a record company for ten years, I had the opportunity to meet many artists, producers and managers, and it has been invaluable to my success as a music publisher. Like you, I am continually making new contacts and opening new doors. I know that it can be very discouraging at times. When I first started pitching songs, I thought I had to connect with every major manager, producer or head of A&R (Artists and Repertoire, the department at record companies with the responsibility of signing new artists and finding songs for the artists on the label). You need to be open to meeting everyone. You also need to learn who is going to be effective for you and who isn't. There are real players and then there are those who only play. You need to nurture the relationships that work for you and not waste time with those that don't.

I had a song plugger tell me of an experience he had with an A&R woman at a major label.

She had an artist who was very hesitant to record outside songs (songs she hadn't written herself). The artist's first album received critical acclaim but was not successful commercially. The A&R woman felt that with a couple of hit outside songs, they could break this artist. For most people, it was very difficult to get this A&R person on the phone, let alone sit down with her in a meeting. Because the song plugger really felt strongly about this particular artist recording his song, he persisted and got a meeting. The A&R woman loved the song he played her. In fact, she even recited the lyric out loud. She told him the song was absolutely perfect and that she would call him the following week, after she played it for the artist. She did not call him that following week, so he continued calling her for several weeks. She never returned his call. He got a friend to get the song to the artist who was on the road. The artist liked the song. The song plugger then sent a letter to the A&R woman stating that he had heard that the artist liked the song, and asked if she or her secretary could get back to him and let him know the song's status. He *never* heard from her or her secretary. Needless to say, the song plugger was outraged. The artist finished the record with no outside songs. The record received critical acclaim but only sold about 18,000 copies. Obviously, there was no point in the song plugger trying to build this relationship. You have to realize that these types of people are a waste of time. No matter how many phone calls you make to them, it won't change how poorly they do their jobs. You can't take it personally. Trying to work with people like this has to be the biggest frustration you will experience in pitching songs. The way to get through these kinds of encounters is to realize that the person is not effective for you and to just move on. There is a happy ending to this story. The song plugger continued to pitch the song and eventually found an artist and producer who believed in it as much as he did. They recorded it and the song became a Top Ten hit!

Work with people who are serious about results and success, not just the heads of companies but the junior executives as well. Even if they are not in the position to get the song directly to the artist, they may express enough enthusiasm to their boss who can pass it on to the artist. In a year, the junior person could be promoted to be in charge of the entire company. It happens all the time.

## Do Your Homework

There are numerous artists, labels, film and TV projects that are looking for songs. There are always new situations that are opening up. Check with the label's A&R department to find out who is looking for material. Research which artists record outside songs and what kind of songs they prefer. You can find this information out by studying the writers credits on albums and on the charts in *Billboard Magazine* and seeing whether or not the artist is the writer on all of the material. You really need to hone your casting skills. Analyze what subjects and emotions a particular artist likes to sing about. Don't just listen to their last hit. Listen to their last album and try to get a sense of what the artist is about. Some artists are drawn to songs with positive lyrics; others may not record songs with lyrics that are too suggestive. This is information that you need to arm yourself with in order to get results. Obviously, there is no point in pitching an outside song to U2 or Sting. Even if your song sounds as if it would be appropriate for one of these artists, it is extremely unlikely that they would record it since they write all of the material for their records. Let's discuss an artist who does record outside

material and what would be the best approach in pitching your song to them.

Let's use Starship as an example. The first thing you should do is to go back and listen to their last record. This will help familiarize you with what they do. Find out who will be producing the next record. Check with the A&R department of their label, their music publisher, or with anyone you know who had involvement with their last record. You can find out who their record label, music publisher and producer are by getting the album and reading the credits, or by checking the small print on the charts in *Billboard Magazine*. To find out how to contact the appropriate people, the best place to start is by calling the label. The label will most likely have offices in Los Angeles, New York, London or Nashville, and checking the phone book or telephone information will definitely get you going. The same holds true for contacting music publishers. The only way to find out if a particular project is being handled out of the L.A., New York or Nashville office is to take your chances and call one of the label's offices. They will direct you to the proper place. Getting in touch with the producer can be a little more difficult, but a call to the sources I just mentioned will most likely get you a contact number.

Call the producer; if you can't speak to him, talk to his assistant and find out what direction the new record is taking. Will it be more AOR (album-oriented radio) or CHR (contemporary hit radio)? This information will make a big difference in what songs you choose to pitch. Unfortunately, a lot of publishers just send songs that sound like the artist's last record—usually a very nonproductive pitch. This is where you get to be creative.

Imaginative casting can provide artists with songs that enable them to branch out and grow. Sheena Easton is an artist who drastically changed directions from one album, *Do You*, to her next album, *The Lover In Me*. If you had pitched her pop/adult contemporary songs like the songs that were on her previous album for *The Lover In Me*, you would have been totally off the mark. A call to her manager, label or producers would have clearly given you insight into the direction her record was taking. Find out what has already been written for the album. Maybe they have already written their up-tempo material and need a smash ballad, or perhaps they're looking for a duet to finish up the record. Gaining this information will make your pitching easier and more accurate.

Be open to giving songs to new artists. A songwriter, Steve Dorf, told me a great story about a song that he had originally given to Jermaine Jackson to record. Jermaine phoned him for a lead sheet and told him that he wasn't sure if the song was going to make his record but that he had decided to record it as a duet with a new female artist on Arista. Reluctantly, he consented to give his song to this new artist for her debut album. At the same time he wondered, Will this new artist, Whitney Houston, sell any records? Whitney's debut album sold over ten million copies!

Be flexible about the opportunities that are presented to you. If you have a song that you feel is perfect for Aretha Franklin but the A&R person wants to cut it as a single for a new artist, don't discount the potential of having a hit. What if the new artist was Wilson Phillips? Find out more about the artist. Do they have strong management? Who is producing the record? Listen to a tape of what has already been recorded. Ask to see a photo. Do they have an image that is marketable? Now, you get to play the role of A&R. It's okay to hold out for a stronger artist, if you have really researched the new artist and you don't believe they have what it takes to be successful, but it would be a big mistake to disregard a new artist without doing your homework.

It's great for your credibility to have been part of breaking a new artist's career, and it will mean a lot more than just having an album cut on an established artist's record. In addition, if you are part of a new artist's initial success, you will have

an inside track on future recordings by that artist. If you are a writer trying to break into production, you will have a much better chance of producing your hit song on a new artist, rather than on an established act.

Other often overlooked opportunities for cuts are established artists who may not be currently in favor. There are the obvious artists that are continually on the charts like Madonna, who we all would love to have record our songs. But what about those artists that seem to have fallen from grace and have not had a hit in years? Who would have known how hugely successful Tina Turner's album *Private Dancer* was going to be? Look at Donny Osmond's recent success. How about Bonnie Raitt? My point is that you need to be open and in touch with each situation in order to make the right choices for you and your songs.

Other lucrative areas to explore for getting your songs cut are through films and TV. Find out what projects are currently in the works at the film companies and TV networks. Read the trade magazines such as *The Hollywood Reporter* and *Variety*. *The Hollywood Reporter* has weekly listings of films just completed and still under production. They give you the names of all the key people involved in making the film. You can also purchase an annual directory called *Studio Blu-Book* that lists television and film producers, animation companies, actor and celebrity contacts and much more. Call the film companies and TV music departments and try to get the scripts of their current projects. As you're reading, think of what material you may already have that would be applicable to the project. If you feel you have something strong or have an idea for a piece of music, call the music department and ask to speak to the person in charge of picking the music. Tell them that you read the script and that you feel you have something that would work for their project. They will most likely ask you to get it to them. If they like what you've sent them, they'll get back to you and let you know if they want to use your song. Even if your song is not right for a particular project, if they like what you've done, you will have established a new contact that may bear fruit in the future.

You have to be aggressive — determined but not overly pushy. That will irritate them and defeat your whole purpose. If you can get a film company excited about a song, they will usually help with finding the right artist to record it for the film. In television, there are many soap operas, sitcoms and dramatic series that use new music on a regular basis. Making contacts in the film and TV music departments can be extremely beneficial. It may take a while to develop those relationships, but they are well worth it because they are so lucrative. Call the music department periodically to nurture your relationship with your contact there. Continue to send in your material when you feel it is appropriate for a project. If a relationship continues to grow, they will call you when they are looking for material. If they are actually soliciting material from you, you stand a much better chance of something actually making it. Although this area can be very profitable, it is extremely competitive and unpredictable. For most film and TV projects the music is the last thing they have had success with in the past.

## Where to Go for Help

Although the music business can seem almost impossible to break into, there are ways to get your foot in the door. Some books and magazines with invaluable directories list the various record companies, producers, managers and song publishers. Some of these are: *Songwriter's Market*, *Attn: A&R*, *New on the Charts* and *Music Connection*. The performance rights organizations, ASCAP (American Society of Composers Authors and Publishers) and BMI (Broadcast Music Incorporated) can be very helpful in steering you in the right direction. Since they are in competition with each other, they are quite eager to help talented new writers. They each have offices in Los Angeles, New York and Nashville. You can also contact the various songwriter organizations in

your area. There are a few that I would like to recommend to you, such as: LASS (Los Angeles Songwriter's Showcase); NAS (National Academy of Songwriters); and NSAI (Nashville Songwriters Association International). They will not only give you information as to who is looking for material, but will often have meetings where producers or A&R reps listen to tapes. Steve McClintock and Tim James, who wrote "All This Time," a hit for Tiffany, met her producer through LASS. This was a seven-year-old song. If you do not live in Los Angeles, where LASS and NAS are based, or in Nashville, which is headquarters for NSAI, you can mail in your tape. Their reps also travel to various markets where they hold seminars. Prominent producers, managers and A&R reps, to whom you may not ordinarily have access, donate their time to be guest speakers for their panels. There is a fee to join each of these organizations, and you should contact them directly for that information.

## Attitude

Your attitude is a very important factor in pitching songs. You have to have conviction. Your excitement and belief in a song will make a difference. You need to project a positive and confident image which will be a major key to your success. If you are unsure, you can't expect the person you are playing it for to feel any different. Unfortunately some young publishers are more interested in getting to meet with the head of A&R than in the real purpose of the meeting . . . to pitch songs! They don't want to show too much excitement for fear that if the A&R person doesn't like the song, their credibility may be in question. *You* have to believe the song that you're promoting is a hit, and if they pass on it, that's okay. Believe that through perseverance you'll find the right home for the song. There are many examples of songs that took years of pitching before becoming hits. The number one duet, "I Knew You Were Waiting," performed by George Michael and Aretha Franklin, was a four-year-old song. "Don't

Know Much," performed by Linda Ronstadt and Aaron Neville, was over six years old before it was recorded by these artists. The hit "Second Chance," recorded by Thirty-Eight Special, was a four-year-old song that was pitched to the artist. Two of the band members rewrote parts of the song to make it fit their style more closely. Fortunately, most hit songs don't take this long to get cut. If you believe in a song, you should continue to pitch it. Don't give up! Although musical styles change, a hit song will hold up. If it's an older song, you may have to re-demo it to make it sound current. A hit will always be a hit. It's a matter of approaching the right artist at the right time.

In most cases, if you are the writer it's much more difficult to pitch your songs and to hear the criticisms that may be given. This is your art. It would be natural to take it personally if someone didn't like your song. You created it, but you have to be objective about the comments that you get. Imagine that you are representing someone else's work and see if the criticisms make sense when you put a little distance there. If you hear some truth in the criticisms that are given, be professional enough to recognize the opportunity to improve your work. Rewriting is a necessary part of the growth process that will enable you to become a better writer.

Many writers have expressed to me their frustration at having to play their songs to A&R people or producers who they feel have very little talent. Even though you don't verbalize those feelings during the meeting, it will affect the outcome and will block you from really developing a business relationship. Let go of all of those negative thoughts and focus on getting your song to the right artist.

When a writer promotes his own song, it may be more difficult to convince the A&R person that the song is a hit. The A&R person will naturally assume that the writer thinks it's a hit because he wrote it. This situation will change after you have had a few hits. Then they will listen because they don't want to pass up your next hit. In the meantime it's necessary to develop a thicker skin with regard to the inevitable criticism and rejection that you will encounter. Diane Warren, currently one of the most successful writers, told me of a meeting she experienced earlier in her career. The person she was playing her songs to was rocking back and forth in his chair and seemed to really be enjoying the music. She said that in her head she was counting the money she was going to make. Then, after playing a few more of her songs, he stopped the tape and told her he couldn't listen any longer, that her songs were giving him the hives. Can you imagine how she felt?

Always remember, it's just one person's opinion. The next person you meet with could love the song and have the perfect artist to cut it. A positive attitude can make all the difference in enabling you to stay with it long enough to get results. What will determine your success will be:

- Your perseverance
- Your belief
- Your conviction
- Your timing
- Your talent for recognizing hits
- Your ability to cast the songs appropriately

## Meetings vs. Mailing Your Tapes

I have found that 80 percent of my cuts have been as a result of a face-to-face meeting. This should be your first choice. You learn more about the person's ears in a meeting; you will see what he reacts to and what loses his attention. For instance, there is a very prominent A&R person who doesn't like songs that mention the title in the beginning of a song. There are many *hits* that have the title in the first line. Classics such as "Yesterday," "Only You," "Feelings" and "Help" are but a few. An example of a current hit would be "Janie's Got a Gun," by Aerosmith. It's all very subjective. He is an A&R person whom I like and with whom I have gotten cuts. I don't waste his time or mine by playing him songs that he will not relate to. How did I learn this? In my first meeting with him, I played a song with the title in the first line. He stopped the song halfway through the chorus and told me that he didn't like songs with that kind of format.

If I believed in my heart that this song was perfect for an artist on his label, I would send it to the producer and manager of the artist as well. But it's important to be respectful. If the A&R person is someone with whom you have a strong relationship, you should ask him if he would mind if you sent it to the other people involved in the project, because if the artist likes it, they will eventually make him aware of where they got the song. You don't want him to feel that you went around him. First consideration should be given to those with whom you have long-term relationships.

There is another A&R person who is known to be a real "song person," who doesn't like song demos that are heavily produced. He always responds more strongly to my songs that have a simple demo. Such an A&R person is rare, however. For most people, you need to spell out as much as possible, which requires that more attention be given to the production. It is, however, a fine line. You want the demo to have a strong impact and stand out, yet you don't want to stylize it to the point of limiting your cuts. If the guitars are too heavy, for example, it could be harder to pitch a song as pop; the listener might regard it as being too rock. Sometimes writers add instruments for color, but a listener could get stuck hearing a particular instrument rather than the overall song.

There is another A&R person at a major label who reacts to a song based on the bridge. He says the bridge determines, for him, whether the song is a hit or not. Once again, it is all very subjective. Knowing their preferences will allow you to be more effective at pitching songs to them. Often, in a meeting, an A&R person or producer will let you know about other artists who are looking for material. In addition, they will tell you about fu-

ture projects, which, if you are a writer, will give you a chance to write specifically for an artist.

Earlier we discussed networking and building relationships. Meetings are a big part of these two elements. Once you have established a strong relationship, it is not necessary to meet every single time you have a new song. You can occasionally mail a tape. You have already earned their respect and they will be eager to hear it. Arranging a meeting with some industry people will be virtually impossible. But try, at least, to speak to them on the phone or make their assistant aware that a package is on its way. Always send your tape to the attention of a specific person, because most major companies will not open unsolicited packages. Be sure to include a lyric sheet; it will help focus the listener's attention. In your cover letter, specify which artists you feel the song would be strong for and mention any past successes or background information that will strenghten your position. Limit the number of songs you send to three or four. Any more than that and you will more than likely lose their interest. One essential requirement in pitching songs by mail or through a meeting, is following up. Most of the cuts that I've gotten through mailing a tape were as a result of my calling to make sure the appropriate person heard the song. In most cases, prior to the call they had not listened to it. The call prompted them to actually play the tape. If you don't hear from someone you sent a tape to, you can't assume that they listened to it and didn't like it. More than likely, they haven't had a chance to review it. Your phone call will bring attention to the tape and they will usually sort it out from the pile and give it a listen.

## Holds

When you have a song that an artist, producer or A&R person feels is a hit, you will be asked for a "hold," (a verbal agreement that you will no longer pitch the song to other artists). The artist will have an exclusive right for a certain amount of time to record the song.

When do you give a hold and for how long? Each situation is different. It has been my experience that the longer the hold the less likely the song will be recorded. Preferably, a hold should not be given until after the artist has heard the song and expressed a desire to record it.

Most producers, managers and A&R people understand this. They realize that it is unfair to hold a song for an artist who has not yet heard the song, because this could prevent you from taking advantage of other opportunities. There is no guarantee that their artist will even like the song, so it doesn't make sense to give them a hold until you have a firm commitment from the artist. Unfortunately there are a few producers and A&R people who will demand a hold instantly. You will have to decide if it is worth it to you or not. Obviously, you will base this decision on the producer's track record and credibility and who the artist is. I don't know anyone who would not give an instant hold to Clive Davis (president of Arista Records).

There are a rare few who are in the position to convince an artist to record a song that they believe in. They are usually very respectful to writers and publishers because they know that by maintaining those relationships, they will get to hear the best material before anyone else. They are also very honest regarding the status of the project along the way. That is all you can ask for.

*Timing* is an important and often underestimated factor in pitching songs. I no longer pitch songs at the beginning of a project. Often, this is the stage where they haven't quite settled on what they are looking for. If the artist writes, they aren't usually very open to outside songs. The producer will give the artist a certain amount of time to see what he or she can create, without forcing the artist to rely on other writers. I continually check in to see at what stage the project is. If there is still a need for outside songs, after the artist has spent ample time writing, that would be the best time to start pitching songs. You will know in a relatively short amount of time whether the song

is going to be recorded or not, which minimizes the amount of time your song is put on hold.

I would like to share with you one of my learning experiences in relation to holds. I had a song on hold with a producer for the group Heart to record. This producer kept the song on hold for eight months. Normally, I would never give a hold for that amount of time, but Heart was the perfect artist for the song. The writer or I would check in regularly with the producer to find out the status of the song. During every call we were told that the song was a smash and to hang in there. There were two other artists who wanted to record the song, but we honored the hold. Heart did not cut the song. A friend of mine from Nashville came to town and played them a song at the very end of the project. They had already cut fourteen songs, but her song happened to be what they had decided was missing from the overall feel of the record. They recorded *her* song. Sadly, other writers I know who had songs recorded by Heart did not make the record. This was a tough call. I eventually told the producer that I was disappointed that he had held the song for so long and didn't even attempt to cut it. Because of this I also told him that I was no longer sending him songs. He explained his situation, and we worked it out. We now have a mutual respect and understanding. I continue to send him songs, and he is very honest about the status of projects on which he is working. Because we both plan to be in this business for a long time, it was necessary for us to resolve the problem. My talent is picking hits and casting them for the right artists. His talent is producing great records. I have no doubt that we will share success together. The song I have been discussing is now on hold for another major artist. Needless to say, I am monitoring the situation very closely!

Once you decide to give a hold, you must honor your commitment. When I was in A&R at RCA, there was a song on hold for the group Five Star. There were two writers of the song and two publishers. Our A&R man in England requested the hold since he was the executive producer of the record. The producer that he was going to hire to record the song with Five Star was also producing Starship. Before the producer was told the song was on hold for Five Star, the other publisher played it to him for Starship. He loved the song and wanted to cut it with Starship, which was his current project. The original publisher who gave a hold for Five Star really wanted the Starship cut, but did not want to hurt his relationship with the A&R person he had originally given a hold to. The other publisher did not care. He just wanted what he thought was a better cut. He was going to let Starship record the song. The only reason that this worked out fairly is because both artists were on RCA. My boss and I were very involved in selecting songs for Starship. We told both publishers that they had to honor the hold for Five Star and that we would not condone giving the song to Starship.

If the two artists had been on different labels, the outcome would have been much different. The publisher would have gone for the artist he thought would be a better cut—Starship—with no regard for the original artist or A&R person to whom they had given a hold. This would have been a very foolish move. You can't afford to burn bridges like this. Despite its apparent size, it's really a very small business. No one will want to deal with you if you don't keep your word. When you have a good reputation your contacts continue to grow!

If the songs you are promoting have another publisher involved, it is important to communicate with the other publisher other serious interest you have received on a song. If you are the publisher or song plugger, you should discuss any interest the song has received with your writer before giving an official hold. He or she should discuss it with the co-writer. If you have a relationship with the co-publisher, you should contact them. If not, make sure that the co-writer advises his publisher. This is essential. The co-writers and co-publishers are also working to get

the song cut. The last thing you want to happen is to give a hold to Paula Abdul and then have the other publisher give it to an unknown, mediocre artist. You cannot refuse to let an artist record a song if the other publisher is willing to grant a license. Not only would you lose the cut, but you would hurt your credibility as well. Most co-publishers are very cooperative. Their goals are the same as yours. They want the best cut for the song.

You need to check on the status of your holds on a regular basis. People will tell you that your song is a definite cut, but the truth is that the situation can change at any moment and during any phase of the project. Recording dates could get delayed. In the meantime, the artist may decide to write more for the record or a writer who has had tons of success could play the artist a song that could knock yours off the record. These are the realities of pitching songs. That is why timing is so important and why you need to know what is going on at all times with the record. If you feel the interest is less, you need to aggressively start finding a new home for the song.

## The Presentation

When making your presentation, there are many areas to consider:

- Your image
- Demo decisions
- Focusing the listener
- How many songs to play

A president of a publishing company once confided in me that he was considering letting his vice-president go. One of his biggest complaints was the way the vice-president dressed. His usual attire was a t-shirt, jeans and tennis shoes. The president felt that this was inappropriate to wear at meetings with heads of film companies, attorneys and other high-powered industry people. He didn't feel the vice-president projected an image of success. I felt he was being a bit extreme to consider firing him, but I do agree that how you dress is a reflection of who you are. If you look successful, you'll feel more confident and will be taken more seriously. Remember, this is a job of selling. Obviously you are not required to wear a suit and tie in the record business and you shouldn't, but your clothes do make a statement. If you are a songwriter and you are trying to break into production, your image could have an impact. If you look like a struggling writer, that's usually how you will get treated. If you have had a bit of success and look hip, the image you are presenting is that you are on the verge of even more success. This, along with your hit song, could make all the difference. People may not even be consciously aware of making these judgments, but they do. Once you have had five number one hits, this does not apply. You are instantly accepted and regarded as talented no matter what. Of course, in order to maintain this status, you have to keep having hits.

Another important aspect to consider is your demo production. The two most critical areas to focus on are the lead vocal and the feel. Make sure that the lead vocal is out front and that the feel is just right for the song. If you are not a musician, hire someone who can create the feel you are looking for. Choosing the right vocalist to communicate your song is crucial. It is generally a mistake to choose a singer who sounds like an imitation of the artist that you are pitching the tune to. Not only will this limit your cover possibilities, because you have aimed it at one specific artist, but it will turn off the original artist that you were hoping would record your song. No artist likes to hear a poor copy of himself.

On the other hand, if you are a writer and sing, that doesn't mean your voice will have the most impact for selling your song. Learn what style of music you sing best, and use your voice on those types of songs. Be aware of the various singers that are available to hire for your demos. The vocalist can make a big difference. If you are not aware of vocalists in your area for a particular style of music, check with other writers you know who write in that genre and check the clubs that cater to that type of music. You can also contact the local AFTRA (American Federation of Television and Radio Artists—a performer's union) chapter for recommendations.

Another way to increase your chances of getting a cut is to really focus the listener on who might be able to shine, as an artist, by performing your song. We have already discussed how essential it is to develop your casting skills. If a person likes a song but really doesn't have a particular artist to record it, more than likely the song will be put to the side. This is where you can be very creative. Let's say you are meeting with a producer. If you come up with a great casting idea for a song, often the producer will send it to that artist or label as an enticement to let him produce the act. If your song helps him to secure work, he will certainly call you when he is looking for songs for future projects. You have to be resourceful and constantly think of new ways to get your songs heard by the right people.

When I was in A&R at RCA, I received an invitation from an artist to have a gourmet meal delivered to my office. A waiter came to my office with a videocassette. He turned on the video, and as the waiter poured me a glass of wine, a waiter on the video poured a glass of wine for the artist. The artist introduced himself and thanked me for listening to his material. I was served an elaborate meal as the artist continued on video to perform two songs.

Your idea doesn't have to be as costly as that, but it helps if you can come up with a clever approach. I was interviewed for a magazine once and I mentioned that I like to cook. Weeks after the article came out, I received a few tapes with gourmet cookbooks. They did stand out from all of the other tapes!

We've talked about your image, the priorities when making your demo and focusing the listener on what artist should cut your song. Now, let's delve further into your actual meeting. Knowing how many songs to play may seem like a minor point, but it's not. Be very selective as to what you play and be aware of the listener's immediate needs. He or she is going to be most anxious to find songs for those artists who are in preproduction and who have not chosen all of their material. You become valuable to them when you provide what they are looking for. If you don't have a song that is really appropriate, don't play a song just to play a song. That will weaken your position and make them doubt your ears. If you have a brand new song that you feel is a hit, let them know that you are excited about the song. Acknowledge that it is not right for the artist for whom they are looking for songs, but that you want them to be the first to hear it. They are usually very receptive to this approach. Even if they don't have anyone to cut it, they may give you great casting ideas for the song. You can usually get a feel for the listener's attention span—which can certainly vary. There is no point in playing a person another song once he has reached saturation. Be aware of this. It's not fair to the song or to the listener. It's much smarter to hold the song for your next meeting.

## Expanding Your Markets

Traveling to another market is always a learning experience. It gives you a different perspective and challenge. In addition, you are opening up new doors and establishing relationships that you will keep for your entire career.

I have spoken to publishers in Los Angeles when they were going through a bit of a lull. A remedy for their situation was to take a trip to Nashville or New York. Each time that I have spoken to them upon their return, they have had a new energy and excitement for what they do. It's like recharging one's batteries. Also, when you are out of your environment, there are no distractions. You have a purpose and a focus. You spend more concentrated time really meeting people and playing songs. ASCAP or BMI may be very helpful in setting you up with appointments in other markets. You need to study the various markets to know what kinds of music they relate to.

If you study the international charts in *Billboard*, it will be clear that certain markets have a large audience that prefer dance music, such as France, or that certain markets prefer rock, such as Germany. It is very difficult to get a rock song cut in England. You will learn all of this information by studying the charts and listening to music from their markets. Even if you're unable to travel to these markets, learning about their styles of music will help you to pitch your songs more accurately through the mail. You can call the A&R departments at the record labels, in whatever music center is nearest you (i.e., Nashville, L.A. or New York) to find out the names and addresses of their foreign A&R reps and offices.

When I first started my publishing company, I had a writer confide in me that she was fed up with the record business and thinking of throwing in the towel. She was seriously thinking of even moving out of Los Angeles. She had previously been a staff writer with a major publisher. We set up a time to get together so that I could listen to her songs, with the hope that I could help encourage her in some way. We listened to about twelve songs, ranging from country, to pop, to R&B. The songs were average with the exception of one song which was magical. I was so thrilled that she had written this song. Her spirits were uplifted by my enthusiasm and belief in her talent. I picked up the song for my publishing company. The song had a bit of racial controversy in the lyric which made it very difficult to get cut. I played this song for over two hundred people. A lot of people were stirred emotionally by the song, but they were afraid of it. Other people felt that it was so artistic, that the kind of artist who would record it would be an artist who writes himself and that would not do outside material. On a trip to London I played the song for a producer, who at the time had the number one record on the U.S. charts. He begged me not to play the song for another person and swore that he would cut the song within a year. He is currently in the studio recording this song with a new artist.

There are many markets to explore. Obviously, Nashville is geared more towards country music, but there are outlets for other types of music, too. There are producers who live in Nashville who are also producing pop, rock, gospel and R&B records. Major artists live in Nashville and record there. Nashville is a serious songwriter's town. The producers and A&R people are continually looking for outside material to record and are usually very specific about what they are looking for. You will find they are very accessible and open to hearing songs for their artists.

Before going to any new market, set up as many appointments ahead of time as you can. Obviously, your schedule will change once you are there. You will connect with people who will introduce you to other people. You want to maximize the productivity of your trip.

## Collaborations

Certain types of music, such as rock, are much more difficult to get cut. I promote my rock songs just as much as I promote my songs in other genres. A lot of rock bands are self-contained and prefer to write their own songs. In these situations I push for my writer to collaborate with the artist. If the artist feels that he is part of the song, your chances of the song making the record are greater.

My first priority is to convince the rock artist to cut the song that I believe is a hit for him. My experience has been that most rock artists are more open to collaborations. If the record company doesn't feel that it has a hit with the material that the artist has already written, most artists would prefer writing with an outside writer than cutting an outside song. This is what I mean about being resourceful, by making the situation work for you. It also helps the credibility of the artist, which is what the A&R person and the manager are looking to develop. Sometimes they may be interested in your song but want to change the lyric or music to fit their style more closely. Because it is so difficult to get rock cuts, you need to be open to these kinds of situations.

If you're a lyricist or if you represent one, there are some alternative choices. When trying to reach a specific artist, check to see who wrote most of the music on his last record. Write a great lyric for the artist and make contact with that writer, to see if he would want to write the music. He will already have access to the artist, and you know that it will get a fair listen. In most cases, it is easier to make these collaborations happen when the writer is approached from your publisher. Being represented by a reputable publisher will give a certain amount of credibility to you as a writer. That's not to say if you don't have a publisher that you shouldn't approach them yourself. Unfortunately, unless you have a proven track record it will be much more difficult. This approach also applies for getting a great track to a lyricist who works frequently with a specific artist.

## Publishers/Song Pluggers

Pitching songs is not easy. I want to give you a realistic picture of how difficult it can be to get cuts. It can be tough just getting your tape heard by the people who have the power to decide what gets recorded. Then you have the job of convincing them that your song is a hit. If you look at the *Billboard* Hot 100 Charts, you'll see that typically less than 10 percent of the songs are outside material. Now take into consideration how many publishers there are, how many talented writers are writing, and how many songs are being promoted daily for these artists. You have your work cut out for you.

With this in mind, having a professional song plugger or music publisher represent your songs is worth serious consideration. If you have no previous success as a writer, it can be difficult for you to get meetings with the various A&R reps, managers and producers. That is where a song publisher or song plugger can be invaluable. He or she has earned a certain amount of credibility that enables you to get a foot in the door and get your song heard by the right people. How do you choose the right publisher or plugger? You should base your decision on their belief in you as a writer and their proven track record or reputation within the industry. If they are truly enthusiastic about your talent as a writer, that is how they will promote you. Most new publishers are determined to have success, and they are worth approaching, too.

The song publisher and the song plugger ultimately have the same job, to get your songs recorded, but each has his own set of rules as to what you get and what you give up.

A publisher who signs your song may give you an advance to be applied against your royalties. You may also be reimbursed for part or all of your demo costs. You, in return, will usually be required to give up 100 percent of your publishing. The publisher will own the copyright for the life of the song, except as provided by the copyright law. You will receive the writer's share of earnings of the song, usually 50 percent. This is standard for a beginning writer. As you become more successful you will have more options to choose from, such as a co-publishing deal, an administration deal or even a subpublishing deal for foreign territories. It really doesn't mean anything to hold on to 100 percent of a song that never gets recorded. You have to decide whether you have enough contacts and the ability to do it on your own, or if you need help.

Song pluggers offer many different types of deals. Often they receive a percentage of the income from the specific cut that they generate. You do not receive an advance, but they usually do not make any money until they get you a cut. In some situations they have no copyright participation. Deals can be worked out in which the song plugger will own the copyright after the song reaches a certain chart position or upon getting a cut.

All of these points are negotiable. A disadvantage of signing with a publisher as a staff writer is that they own the copyrights of all your songs during the time of your agreement, whether they get you a cut or not. Publishers will sign a writer on a song-by-song basis, but the advance, if any, will be minimal.

Both the publisher and plugger will give you creative feedback on your songs. They may give you input on how to demo or improve a song. The hit song "Wind Beneath My Wings" was originally conceived by the writers as an up-tempo song. It was the publisher who suggested they rearrange it as a ballad. Not all publishers or pluggers will have this talent. There are those who may try to change things just to be involved. It's important for you to find a publisher or plugger who believes in your talent as a writer and whom you respect enough to take seriously. In the end you will weigh the difference and make the final decisions. The publisher or plugger will also come up with casting ideas and let you know who is currently looking for material. You should continue to pitch songs, even if you have representation. A good publisher or plugger will have a feel for who you might work well with, both musically and personally, and will set up collaborations with those writers to whom you might not have access. Sometimes there might be an area where another writer has a particular strength that you could benefit from. Although you write everything, maybe your strength is lyrics. Putting you with someone whose strength is music may clearly improve a song. At times, publishers and pluggers will put more experienced writers in collaborations with recording artists who need stronger songs. As we discussed earlier, this is obviously an advantage for a writer, because it increases the chances of the song making the record.

If you are a writer with a few hits, established contacts, and financial security, the option of pitching without representation may make sense. Until you reach that point, however, you may want to consider the avenues I've discussed.

## Summary

Pitching songs is hard work but the rewards are well worth it. Nothing is more exciting than putting the right song with the right artist and watching it climb the charts! Belief in the quality of what you have to offer is the driving force behind everything. You can't be stopped if your belief and willingness to learn are stronger than the obstacles that you have to overcome. You need to look at every obstacle that you are faced with as a challenge, and I assure you there will be many. Every rejection teaches you something about yourself, as well as the person for whom you're playing the material. Can you take criticism and grow from it? It's essential to be able to take negative comments constructively, without letting them unnerve you. Everyone is entitled to an opinion. This really is an opportunity for you to gain insight that will make you even more successful in the future. Obviously, not every criticism will be valid. Playing songs for people whom you respect musically can provide you with valuable feedback. If you start getting the same comments from several people, you may want to take a closer look to see if the song can be improved.

Your attitude can make the difference in whether or not you stay with it long enough to get results. I have seen writers, publishers and song pluggers become very bitter and disillusioned regarding the music business and the people whom they have to deal with. They have let their feelings influence their productivity and chances for success.

There is no denying that this business is fraught with many frustrations and unscrupulous people. But what business isn't? The fact that there are no set rules only makes it more exciting. Almost anything that you can dream up, you can make happen. The possibilities are endless. You are not confined to a limited number of artists, producers or record labels, and this should be encouraging. There are so many doors to open and so many opportunities to succeed. If you look at the most successful men and women today in any business, the majority attribute their success to perseverance. Continually nurture the business relationships that you have, and always be open and positive about making new contacts. In the same sense, learn which contacts work for you

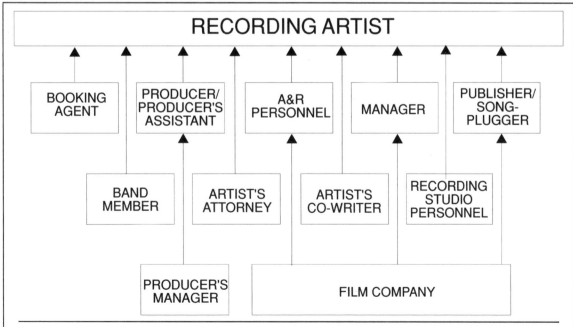

Figure 1. As you can see from this chart, there are many ways to approach an artist. Don't limit yourself by sending your songs only to the A&R person or producer. Explore every possible avenue!

and which don't. Pay attention to the timing of a project. Getting in too early or too late can cost you. When you have a song on hold, relentlessly check on the status of the record, because it constantly changes. Being as knowledgeable as you can about the music business will increase your chances of being successful. Read the various tip sheets and trade magazines. Arm yourself with as much information as you can. Through your own experiences, you will learn even more. See you on the charts!

•   •   •

## Teri Muench

 Teri Muench has over twelve years of record company experience. She was an A&R Director and Executive Producer for RCA Records, working with such artists as Starship, Diana Ross, Rick Springfield, Bruce Hornsby, The Pointer Sisters and Mr. Mister. She is co-author of *Attn: A&R* and has her own successful publishing company, Muench Music Group.

She has found numerous songs for artists to record, including the number one song "Nothing's Gonna Stop Us Now." She has also served as a consultant for various companies such as Chrysalis Records and Famous Music. In addition, she has served on the Board of Governors for NARAS (Grammy Awards).

# Glossary

A&R—Artist and Repertoire, the department or record company employee having the responsibility of finding new artists for the label and outside material that they may record.

AABA—A conventional song pattern consisting of four basic sections, three of which are musically the same and one that is different, such as verse, verse, bridge, verse. Other common patterns are AABB and AABCA. In certain types of contemporary pop music, there has been a trend for songs to be less patterned and structured around repetitive hooks.

ADDITIVE SYNTHESIS—A method of sound generation that uses a series of sine waves (pure tones) at different harmonic intervals (different pitches) summed together to create the sound.

ANALOG SYNTHESIS—A method of sound generation that uses changing voltages to create a sound.

AUDIO SIGNAL—The representation of sound as an electrical impulse.

BOUNCING—The process of consolidating two or more tracks (on a multi-track recorder), by mixing them together and re-recording them on a spare track.

BUS—An electrical pathway through which several channels can be combined.

CHART—A listing of the top-selling and/or most frequently broadcast records of a particular category. Charts are compiled by and published in trade publications.

CHORUS—A delay setting which imitates the effect of a large ensemble.

COLLABORATOR—One who writes a song with another.

COMMERCIAL—A quality of a creative work that is deemed to have mass appeal.

COMPRESSOR—A device which restricts the dynamic range of an audio signal.

DAISY CHAIN—A method of connecting different MIDI instruments together in a chain using a cable plugged into the MIDI OUT port of the first instrument, the other end of which is plugged into the MIDI IN port of a second MIDI instrument. A second cable is plugged into the MIDI THRU port of the second instrument, the other end of which is plugged into the MIDI IN port of a third instrument. Another MIDI instrument may be added to the chain using this method.

DELAY—A device used to introduce a time-lag in the audio signal.

DEMO—A preliminary recording of a song used to show its potential.

DIGITAL DRUM MACHINE—An electronic musical instrument (which usually uses MIDI) that contains the digital representation of many drum and percussion sounds that can be programmed to be played in various rhythmic patterns to create the drum portion of a song.

DIGITAL SYNTHESIS—A method of sound generation that uses binary numbers (0's and 1's) to represent changing values which are then converted into an electrical signal that creates a sound.

DOUBLING—A delay setting that imitates the effect of an additional performance, thereby "doubling" the sound.

DYNAMIC RANGE—The difference between the loudest and softest sound.

ECHO—A sound effect that occurs when there is an audible time lag between the original and the delayed version of a sound.

ENVELOPE GENERATOR—The circuit of a synthesizer that controls the attack time, decay time, sustain level, and release time of a sound.

EQUALIZER—Usually built into a mixer, this device allows one to manipulate the tone of a sound by boosting or cutting particular frequencies or groups of frequencies.

EXPANDER—A device that increases the dynamic range of an audio signal.

FLANGING—A short delay setting that causes

an identifiable "whooshing" effect.

FORMAT—The musical style of particular radio station programs.

HARDWARE—The actual physical devices used in the MIDI setup. These devices include the keyboards, expanders, drum machine, sequencer, computer, etc.

HOOK—A section of a song—a melody and lyric line or an instrumental riff—that repeats throughout the song and captures the listener's attention.

LAWYER—In the music business, lawyers serve to negotiate contracts or advise writers, artists and other creative people of the pitfalls or plusses of contracts offered to them. It's cliché, but it is always best to consult a music business lawyer before signing a contract.

LEAD SHEET—A page with the music and lyrics to a song written on it.

LIMITING—An extreme form of compression that sets a ceiling on the volume of an audio signal, beyond which it cannot go.

LYRIC SHEET—A page on which song lyrics are printed or typewritten.

MASTER—The final, mixed down recording from which duplicates are made.

METAPHOR—The likening of one object to another. In lyric writing, an effective metaphor can express much succinctly; on the other hand, a clichéd metaphor makes the lyric sound trite or jaded.

MIDI—The acronym for Musical Instrument Digital Interface, MIDI is a microprocessor communications network that allows various musical instruments from different manufacturers to be interconnected to form an efficient music-making system.

MIDI CHANNEL—The particular channel that MIDI information is sent and received on. Sixteen MIDI channels are available for the exchange of digital musical information.

MIDI EXPANDER—The nucleus or "brain" of a MIDI keyboard, minus the physical black and white keys.

MIDI IN, OUT, THRU—The receptacles that MIDI cables are plugged into that are used for the exchange of digital musical information.

MIDI MASTER KEYBOARD—The first MIDI keyboard used in a MIDI chain.

MIXER—A device used to route audio signals and/or blend them together before they are recorded.

MODULATION—The ability to electronically and automatically "waver" the pitch (vibrato), the volume (tremolo), or the filter cut-off (wah-wah) of a sound.

MULTI-TRACK TAPE RECORDER—A recording machine capable of recording performances separately on two or more tracks of tape. There are 4-, 8-, 12-, 16-, 24-, and other kinds of multi-track tape recorders.

MUSIC PUBLISHER—A company that finds original songs with commercial potential and gets them recorded. Once recorded, the company will exploit a composition—try to maximize its uses (and income) by obtaining covers and getting it used in motion pictures, jingles and other areas—and handle copyright, financial, and other administrative responsibilities. The person at a music publishing company who signs new writers and compositions may have any of several titles, including professional manager, song plugger or director of creative affairs.

NOISE-GATE—An extreme form of expansion that essentially shuts off a low-level audio signal, opening up only when a strong signal is present.

OVERDUB—The process by which performances are added to basic tracks on a multi-track recording session.

PERSONAL MANAGER—One who guides a recording artist or other creative professional in his professional affairs.

PITCH—To market a song or play it for someone who can record it or get it recorded.

PITCH BEND—The ability to "bend" the pitch of a note(s) higher or lower using a joystick or pitch wheel located on the front panel of a synthesizer.

PREPRODUCTION—For producers and recording artists, preproduction is a stage, prior to going into the studio, during which songs are chosen and worked out for the artist. For songwriters, it is the time before a tune is demoed when the writer strategizes the arrangement and production.

QUANTIZATION — The process of auto-correcting timing mistakes made while using a MIDI sequencer or programming a digital drum machine. This auto fix-it is also referred to as "error-correcting."

RECORD COMPANY — A company that releases and distributes recordings (in formats such as cassettes or compact discs), either through owned branches or by arrangement with independent companies. Major record companies have the internal apparatus to promote, market and distribute recordings or artists on their rosters internationally.

RECORD PRODUCER — The person who supervises the recording of a song. Responsibilities include song selection, overseeing the kind of arrangement used, monitoring the artist's and musician's performances in the studio, communicating to the engineer particular kinds of sounds or effects desired, mixing or overseeing the final mix of the tracks, and handling the paperwork with regard to union regulations.

REVERB — A complex combination of echoes that linger after the original sound has stopped.

SAMPLING — The process of digitally recording a sound that can then be played from a MIDI keyboard in half-step musical intervals that correspond to the black and white keys of the keyboard.

SEQUENCER — A MIDI device that records and plays back digital musical information. It is similar to a multi-track tape recorder, with the exception that the musical information recorded and played back exists strictly in the digital domain.

SOFTWARE — A series of instructions that exist in digital form and are usually stored on a floppy disk. Computer programs are software-based programs.

STEP-TIME PROGRAMMING — The process of entering one note and/or rest at a time into a MIDI sequencer.

STORY SONG — A lyric with a plot and drama. Plot twists and strong chracterization increase the effectiveness of the lyrics.

SYNCHRONIZER — An electrical device that allows a MIDI sequencer to be "locked-up" or synchronized to a multi-track tape machine.

SYNTHESIZER — An electronic musical instrument that creates sounds.

TIME COMPRESSION — The process by which the tempo (speed) of a musical composition can be speeded up without altering the pitch of the composition.

TIME EXPANSION — The process by which the tempo (speed) of a musical composition can be slowed down without altering the pitch of the composition.

TRACK — A path on a multi-track recording tape used to store audio information.

TRADE PUBLICATION — A magazine or newspaper that reports the news of an industry. In the entertainment industry, trade publications such as *Billboard* and *Variety* provide useful information to songwriters.

UNION — In the entertainment business there are a number of unions that serve to provide minimum wages and health and pension benefits for performers. Wages vary according to locality and the type of recording or live music session. Among the unions are AFM, AFTRA, SAG, AGMA and AGVA.

VU METER — A device on a tape recorder or recording console that measures the intensity of a sound in volume units (VU).

# Index

synthesizers
   analog, 49
   digital, 52-53
   filters on, 50-51
   sampling, 53-54
   voltage-controlled, 49

**T**ag, 30
talent, need for, in songwriting, 3
tape
   hiss, 57
   mailing to pitch, 67-68
"Tattoo," 12, 20
Thirty-Eight Special, 67
Tiffany, 66
timing, in pitching songs, 69-70
titles, bad, 13
touch sensitivity, 48
   after-touch, 49
   pressure, 49
   velocity, 48
tracks, 58-59
   basic, 31
   bouncing, 32, 59
   pre-mixing, 32

record level, setting on, 31
Turner, Tina, 65
tweaking, 53

**V**ariety, 65
velocity touch sensitivity, 48
verse, 28
Vezner, John, 11
vibrato, 48
"Vincent" (Starry Starry Night), 8, 18
voltage-controlled synthesizer, 49

**W**hat About the Love," 15
"Where've You Been," 11, 19
Wilson Phillips, 65
"Wind Beneath My Wings," 74
wire, shielding, 27
wiring, home studio, 27
word repetition in songwriting, 13
workshop
   function of, 1
   purpose of, 1

**Z**ones, 56

# OTHER BOOKS TO HELP YOU MAKE
# MONEY AND THE MOST OF
# YOUR MUSIC TALENT

**Songwriters on Songwriting**, edited by Paul Zollo 208 pages/$17.95, paperback
**The Songwriter's Workshop**, edited by Harvey Rachlin 96 pages + 2 cassettes/$24.95, paperback
**Singing for a Living**, by Marta Woodhull 160 pages/$18.95, paper
**Jingles: How to Write, Produce, & Sell Commercial Music**, by Al Stone 144 pages/$18.95, paperback
**Music Publishing: A Songwriter's Guide**, by Randy Poe 144 pages/$18.95, paperback
**Making Money Making Music (No Matter Where You Live)**, by James Dearing 192 pages/$17.95, paperback
**Beginning Songwriter's Answer Book**, by Paul Zollo 128 pages/$16.95, paperback
**Playing for Pay: How To Be A Working Musician**, by James Gibson 160 pages/$17.95, paperback
**You Can Write Great Lyrics**, by Pamela Phillips Oland 192 pages/$17.95, paperback
**Protecting Your Songs & Yourself**, by Kent J. Klavens 112 pages/$15.95, paperback
**Gigging: The Musician's Underground Touring Directory**, by Michael Dorf & Robert Appel 224 pages/$14.95, paperback
**The Craft & Business of Songwriting**, by John Braheny 322 pages/$19.95, hardcover
**The Craft of Lyric Writing**, by Sheila Davis 350 pages/$19.95, hardcover
**Successful Lyric Writing: A Step-by-Step Course & Workbook**, by Sheila Davis 292 pages/$18.95, paperback
**Getting Noticed: A Musician's Guide to Publicity & Self-Promotion**, by James Gibson 240 pages/$12.95, paperback
**The Performing Artist's Handbook**, by Janice Papolos 219 pages/$12.95, paperback
**The Songwriter's Guide to Making Great Demos**, by Harvey Rachlin 192 pages/$12.95, paperback
**Writing Music for Hit Songs**, by Jai Josefs 256 pages/$17.95, hardcover
**Making It in the New Music Business**, by James Riordan 352 pages/$18.95
**The Songwriter's Guide to Collaboration**, by Walter Carter 178 pages/$12.95, paperback
**How to Pitch & Promote Your Songs**, by Fred Koller 144 pages/$12.95, paperback
**1991 Songwriter's Market**, edited by Mark Garvey 528 pages/$19.95, hardcover

A complete catalog of all Writer's Digest Books is available FREE by writing to the address shown below. To order books directly from the publisher, include $3.00 postage and handling for one book, $1.00 for each additional book. Ohio residents add 5½% sales tax. Allow 30 days for delivery.

Writer's Digest Books
1507 Dana Avenue
Cincinnati, Ohio 45207

Credit card orders call TOLL-FREE
1-800-289-0963

Prices subject to change without notice